Smoke and Mirrors:
Financial Myths that Will
Ruin Your Retirement
Dreams

EIGHTH EDITION

Smoke and Mirrors: Financial Myths that Will Ruin Your Retirement Dreams

EIGHTH EDITION

David Trahair, CA

IGUANA

Editor: Lisa Sparks
Book layout design: Greg Ioannou
Cover design: Jane Goodwin

First edition: 2004; reprinted 2004
Second edition: 2005
Third edition: 2006
Fourth edition: 2007
Fifth edition: 2008
Sixth edition: 2009
Seventh edition: 2010
Eighth edition: 2012; reprinted 2014

Cataloguing data to come from Library and Archives Canada.

This is the original print version of *Smoke and Mirrors (eighth edition)*.

Acknowledgements

I loved writing this book, but it wasn't produced by me alone. This book is the result of a team effort.

First and foremost I would like to thank the people at Self-Counsel Press for making this venture such a pleasure. I'd like to start by expressing my sincere gratitude to Judy Brunsek. If not for Judy, this book would not exist. She was the one that showed this rookie writer how to actually get past the idea stage.

I'd also like to thank Richard Day for immediately seeing the potential in my proposal; Catherine Plear for her precise editing; Aaron Morris for his creative flair; Roger Kettyls for spreading the word so well; and most of all, Ruth Wilson for her brilliant editing. She has a knack for taking a somewhat complex issue and stating it cleanly and elegantly. Because of her, there now exists a simple book on how Canadians can get their finances under control. I will always owe a lot to Ruth.

I'd also like to give a big thanks to my dedicated associate, Michael Boyd. His financial and computer knowledge, as well as his attention to detail, were invaluable in helping me make this edition the best so far.

I'm also indebted to Ron Cirotto for sharing his mortgage know-how and his excellent amortization software; Alan Salmon for his help in making the Microsoft Excel tools more self-explanatory and interactive; and Kwok Ho and Chris Robinson for their excellent book, Personal Financial Planning.

Last, but not least, I must thank my dad, Peter, for his never-ending support, and, of course, the lights of my life – my wife, Elaine, and our amazing children, Cassidy and Kyle.

Notice to Readers

PART ONE: UNDERSTANDING AND EXPLODING FIVE BIG MYTHS OF FINANCIAL PLANNING

1. Meet the Myths

Seeing through the Smoke and Mirrors

You may be wondering, "another book on financial planning? What more is there to say? Haven't we heard it all?"

In that lies the problem. Each and every day, we are bombarded by messages from so-called financial advisors, the foot soldiers of the big finance companies, imploring us to secure our financial future by giving them control of our personal finances.

You've heard the pitches:

"Invest in our mutual funds and retire rich!"

"Buy life insurance from us and secure your financial future!"

"Get the loan you need to realize your dreams!"

These pitches are often accompanied by scare tactics:

"Don't you know that you'll need millions of dollars stashed away by the time you retire, or you'll be forced to live in a cardboard box, surviving on macaroni and cheese for the rest of your life?"

The truth is that the people who send these messages are pulling the wool over your eyes. Many of them are merely salespeople offering advice that will benefit themselves – not you. They are in it simply for the commissions.

Take the big banks, for example. They are not in business to secure your happy retirement. Their objective is to maximize the value of their company to keep their shareholders happy. They do this by maximizing their profit. When you bank, invest, or borrow from them, they are making money off you with each and every transaction. Their profit comes from your pocket, and it's eating away at your nest egg each and every hour of every day of your life.

It's time to do something about it all. Something needs to be said to clear the air – to help you – and all Canadians see reality through the smoke and mirrors.

Why Listen To Me?

I wrote this book because I have become increasingly angry about the messages sent by the world of financial planners and others who sell financial products. I have come to the conclusion that most of them are simply wrong, and the strategies they ask us to follow can, in fact, suck the financial life out of us. I felt it was imperative to reveal what I believe to be the truth behind the myths we are asked to believe.

Those are my reasons for writing. But why should you read what I have to say?

First and most important, I am an independent source. I have no vested interest in your investments, or whether you have life insurance, or how large your RRSP is, because I don't sell any of those products.

Second, I have the education and experience necessary to explain what you need to know. I am a chartered accountant by profession and have provided financial services to many different types of businesses and individuals for more than 25 years. My training has given me the necessary tools to make some sense of the many complicated and confusing areas related to personal finances.

I have found that the skills I have developed and honed from years of creating and analyzing the financial statements of a diverse range of businesses translates well to the understanding of personal finances. In my own work and in this book, I have taken all the accounting concepts, principles, and procedures used in successful businesses and applied them to the finances of individuals.

Who Should Read this Book?

If you are independently wealthy, own your own mortgage-free home, have been able to maximize your RRSP contributions, have investments outside your retirement plan, spend less than you make each year, and are totally up to date on your personal income taxes, you won't get much out of this book.

It's for everyone else. If any of the following statements describes you, then you've picked up the right book:

- I know my personal finances need improvement but I just can't find the time to deal with them.
- I have a credit card balance that never seems to go down.
- I have no idea how well my investments are doing.
- I own a really nice house ... with a really big mortgage.

- I'm worried about my kids' education, but paying private school fees or saving for university is just adding to my financial pressure cooker.
- I own a whole life insurance policy, and the payments are killing me.
- I still owe personal income tax from prior years.
- I am a student or a recent university graduate with loans to pay off, and I haven't found a job yet.
- I have no idea how much I spent last year on interest.
- I am self-employed and behind on my personal taxes, HST, GST, and payroll taxes.
- I never seem to be able to come up with the money to make my RRSP contribution unless I borrow it.
- I am not good with numbers.

If any item in this list describes you, don't despair. You're not alone. In fact, I would describe you as the typical Canadian – at least in terms of personal finances. But help is at hand. This book was written to help you.

You may have noticed that the above list doesn't mention anything about income level. That's because earning a significant salary or income, even millions of dollars a year, doesn't necessarily mean you are in good shape financially. In fact, you may be in worse shape than someone with a much lower income, because your high income allows you to borrow easily. You can dig yourself into a very deep debt hole that will be extremely tough to get out of if your income is ever significantly reduced. If you fall into this camp, you too should benefit from the words that follow.

How this Book Will Help You

Reading this book and using the tools that you can get free from my website at www.trahair.com will give you what you need to take control of your personal finances, and that's something that most people never do. Many, if not most, people simply give up and assume that their money will "sort itself out in the end."

Nothing could be further from the truth. If you don't take control, someone else will, and that could cost you and your family big time.

There are lots of reasons why so many Canadians have become dependent on the financial advice of the "experts" instead of controlling their own financial decision-making. Let's look at the three main reasons, and how the financial companies feed on them:

• *Lack of financial knowledge:* You may be very good at what you do – whether you are a plumber, a doctor, a professional athlete, or something else – but you probably don't have much training in personal financial matters. If you're like most people, you've probably learned what you do know about finances from your parents, or perhaps from whatever reading you have done during your spare time. The financial companies, however, have thousands of employees trained in finance constantly working on developing products that will make them money. Many of these products are exceedingly complex and are designed in such a way that you may never be able to figure out whether or not they are good for you. Advantage: theirs.

• *Lack of time:* How much time did you spend tracking and analyzing your spending last year? When you last renewed your mortgage, how many hours did you spend researching alternatives? When that life insurance salesperson tried to sell you a whole life policy, did you have it analyzed by an independent professional? There simply aren't enough hours in the day to do all that we need to do in our busy lives. Unfortunately, unless you set priorities to start devoting at least some time to your personal finances, one day it will be too late. Your income will stop but the bills won't. The financial companies know this, and make promises to make it simple and solve your problems. So you end up buying investments you don't understand with fees you don't even see. What are the odds that will work out for you? Advantage: theirs.

• *Not having the right tools:* Even if you do have the financial expertise as well as the time, you may not have the right tools to make an effective decision about your finances. For example, if you are trying to decide whether to lease or buy a car, you may have the figrues, but do you know how to use a business calculator to determine which option is better? When you consider your mortgage options, can you produce an amortization schedule for each one to see which one will cost you the least in interest and allow you to pay off your debt the earliest? (Both these tools are explained in Part Two of this book.) Advantage: theirs.

The large financial institutions invest millions of dollars developing advertising campaigns designed to toy with our emotions and deftly pick our pockets as a result of our not having the knowledge, time, and tools to control our own finances. To sell insurance, they tempt us with early retirement thoughts; to make investments look attractive, they use seductive pictures such as a pristine cottage on a glassy lake or a luxury car. Who can resist?

This book will help you get on track toward controlling your own finances and resisting the siren call of the big financial companies.

What's Between the Covers?

This book is meant for you, the typical Canadian. It's not meant for the bankers, brokers, credit card companies, and certain financial planners and insurance agents. In fact, many of those people are not going to like what they read here, because it counters the advice they give to people every day. But for you, all the content in the following chapters is positive. It will give you the ammunition you need to fight back against the scare tactics and "rule of thumb" selling methods used to suck the money out of your pockets every day of your life.

The remaining chapters in Part One of this book expose the five key myths used by many financial advisors to secure their own financial futures by tricking you into giving them a pipeline to your hard-earned money:

• *Myth 1: If I had $1,000,000 ... I could retire.* The myth that you need more than a million dollars to retire comfortably is a blatant attempt to grab more of your money. That's because the more money you hand over to your investment advisor, the more money he or she makes through commissions and other fees. In Chapter 2, I debunk this myth by using the ultimate weapon – personal financial tracking. I use a fictitious family, the Harts, to show you how to crunch real numbers to prove you need far less than many financial advisors would have you believe.

• *Myth 2: RRSPs are the Holy Grail of retirement.* While an RRSP plays an important part in achieving financial security, there is something far more important to address: how to deal with your debt (e.g., credit card balance, home mortgage, personal line of credit). In Chapter 3, I provide a no-risk strategy that will let you eliminate all your debt, including your mortgage, years before you retire.

• *Myth 3: Don't worry about your investments; you'll be fine in the long run.* The standard message for years has been to trust in the stock market because the average rate of return on stocks, in the long term, will be much better than that of fixed income products such as GICs (guaranteed investment certificates) and term deposits. But what many financial advisors don't reveal is the one simple figure you need: the personal rate of return you are making on your investment portfolio. And why don't they show you this figure? Because it's simply too hard for them to calculate? Or because it would be too "confusing" to explain that your return was actually only 2 percent last year? Maybe it's because they don't want you to know. In Chapter 4, you'll learn how to calculate your own personal rate of return on any investment portfolio using a simple spreadsheet that you can get free from my website (I'll tell you how to do that in a minute). All you need are the dates and amounts of money you invested and the current market value. You can take the results to your next meeting with your advisor and start having some useful discussions.

• *Myth 4: We have met the enemy, and he is the tax collector.* No one likes to pay taxes, and financial salespeople know it. But if you follow the advice many offer – to invest in a tax shelter, or to borrow to invest, for example – in order to lower your tax bill, you may end up broke. In Chapter 5, I use some real-life examples to prove my point: trying to avoid taxes often results in lousy financial decisions and sometimes personal financial disaster.

• *Myth 5: Secure your financial future: Buy life insurance.* Let's face facts. Having a life insurance policy on your own life won't do anything to secure your financial future: you'll be dead if it pays off. Life insurance does, however, serve a purpose. It should help your dependents maintain their standard of living after you are gone. But that's not what you'll hear from many insurance salespeople. Instead you'll hear wonderful things about whole life insurance and how you can save money at the same time you insure your life! It's what they don't tell you that's dangerous to your financial well-being. Chapter 6 reveals the true cost of life insurance and includes step-by-step instructions to help you determine how much coverage you need.

I learned about these myths the hard way – by making the mistakes of following many of them. I exposed the myths by doing my own personal financial tracking. The experience I have gained in doing so is the basis of my opinions in Chapters 2 to 6. It is my hope that you can use my experience to help yourself in your own personal financial planning.

Part Two of this book will help you take the next step. It focuses on saving you thousands of dollars by showing you how to choose the right tools, understand mortgages (likely the largest investment you'll ever make), and decide between leasing or buying a car (one of the other major expenses you may need to consider). It also describes in detail how to track your finances – giving you the ultimate weapon in fighting back. Finally, it summarizes everything you'll have learned by that point and starts you in the right direction for the future.

The Free Tools

If you go to my website at www.trahair.com and click on "Smoke and Mirrors" on the left side you will see all the tools that you can download for free. These Microsoft Excel spreadsheets are an integral part of this book and I encourage you to use them to arm yourself with the information only you can determine. Here's what you get:

• *The Personal Rate of Return Calculator:* Figure out what rate of return your RRSP has generated, then look at the rate on your debt to figure out how much further ahead you'll be by paying off your loans.
• *The Retirement Optimizer:* Simply answer some basic questions to determine how much your RRSP will be worth when you want to retire, whether or not you can afford to retire early, how much retirement savings you will be forced to withdraw each year, whether or not that will result in Old Age Security clawbacks, whether you will run out of money before you retire and much more.
• *My Net Worth Calculator:* Find out this important figure in personal finances: the one that tells you what you are worth.
• *Car Lease versus Buy Analyzer:* Makes it easy to compare and decide how to pay for your next car.
• *My Income and Expenses:* Punch in your monthly expenses and instantly see what your annual expenses are likely to be.
• *Cash Flow Projector:* If you have actual results, use this tool to allocate your spending and reach your goals.

After you've finished reading the book, why not drop by my website at www.trahair.ca to let me know what you think? Has your investment advisor done a great job with your money? If you are already retired, have you found you really do need more than a million dollars tucked away to retire comfortably? Has a life insurance strategy worked well in your family? This is the best information I can get – direct feedback from people with real life experiences. Your comments will help me develop future books that will help others discover the real truth about personal finances.

2. Myth 1: If I Had $1,000,000 ... I Could Retire

Exposing the Myth

The Barenaked Ladies may not have been thinking about retirement when they wrote their popular song "If I Had a Million Dollars," but they could have been, based on the myth perpetuated by the financial community that you will need 70 percent of your final pre-retirement income to maintain your standard of living after you retire. If that were true, it would mean that you would probably need to build up more than a million dollars in investments to earn the required income.

Most financial advisors perpetuate this myth because the more money you hand over to them, the more money they make through commissions and other fees. I have even heard some of them dismiss the Canada Pension Plan (CPP) and Old Age Security (OAS) pension out of hand, as if there is no chance of these plans surviving until you retire. "Better crank up your savings instead," they warn.

Can We Rely on the CPP and OAS Pensions?

First of all, the Canada Pension Plan is not run by the big financial institutions. The responsibility for its operation rests jointly with the federal and provincial ministers of finance. It is financed through mandatory contributions from employees, employers, and self-employed Canadians. The government sets the contribution rates and ensures that employees and employers pay their fair share through payroll deductions and, in the case of the self-employed, through personal income tax returns.

Canada's chief actuary is required to produce an actuarial report every three years to ensure that the plan will be able to fund existing and future retiring Canadians. The last report was in 2009, and it confirmed that a 9.9 percent contribution rate should sustain it over the long term. The results were also reviewed by a team of independent actuaries, and they agreed with the conclusions.

To ensure the investments of the CPP are being handled effectively, the CPP Investment Board was created in 1997 to invest funds not required to pay current benefits. It operates at arm's length and carefully monitors the asset allocation and returns of the investments.

The CPP reserve fund assets were $161.6 billion at March 31, 2012 up from $148.2 billion at March 31, 2011. While continuing to make good investment returns will be a challenge for the CPP, it seems quite solid to me. The Old Age Security pension is not based on employment earnings. It's paid out of current government tax revenues and begins at age 65. The government recently passed legislation to delay the starting age to 67, but can you imagine the revolt if they said they were going to get rid of it altogether? Right – it's not very likely.

The next time your advisor dismisses the CPP and OAS plans, review the facts and ask him or her exactly why he or she has more confidence in his or her own ability to take care of your retirement.

Myth versus Reality

Many people base their current financial goals on when they think they are going to retire and how much money they assume they will need. Everyone has a different retirement dream: some may want to continue working until they drop; others desire to be financially independent by age 55 and spend the rest of their days on a beach. Whatever your plan, you want to avoid the common financial traps that may ruin your dreams.

The actual amount of money you need to save depends less on the 70 percent formula and more on your spending habits, debt levels, and future investment rates of return; that is, the percentage by which your investments grow each year, and the rate they'll pay after you retire. The problem is that nobody can accurately predict what the future will bring. Will the Toronto Stock Exchange, for example, continue to earn about 8 percent a year, as it has over the last 50 years? And, more importantly, what will your rate of return be on the investments you choose to make?

Your Investment Options

When it comes to deciding where to invest your money, you have several basic options: equities (stocks), bonds, and fixed-income products (term deposits, GICs, etc.). Equities are the riskiest, and fixed-income products are the most secure. However, you will pay for security with lower rates of return. The upside is that you generally won't suffer from a decline in value with fixed-income products.

David Trahair

Judging Your Comfort Level

If you want to achieve a higher rate of return than that which fixed-income products can offer, you'll have to accept a greater degree of risk that your investments may decline in value. A lot of people learned that lesson during the stock market crash of 2008-2009. There were many people who lost up to 50 percent of their entire investments in less than a year.

If the thought of losing money makes your stomach churn, investing in the stock market may not be for you, no matter what your age. If that's your situation, don't invest in stocks. There's absolutely nothing wrong with that decision. Whatever you decide, you want to be able to sleep at night. Be prepared, however, for a lower rate of return.

Calculating a Realistic Rate of Return

With retirement planning, it's best to be conservative when choosing a rate of return. Assuming you will make a 10 percent return may give you a warm feeling, but you will find yourself significantly short of retirement funds if actual results turn out to be much lower.

In this book, I have chosen to assume that the future may not be as rosy as the past, and that as you approach retirement, you will need to reduce your exposure to risk by switching to lower rate fixed-income investments. Therefore, in the examples in this book I use an average annual rate of return of 5 percent. When doing your own analyses, you should use a rate that reflects your own beliefs and attitudes toward risk tolerance.

Debunking the Rule of 70 Percent

Consider this example: assume that the year before you retire, your combined household income is $100,000. The rule of thumb says you will need 70 percent of your pre-retirement income, or $70,000 per year during retirement to maintain your lifestyle. Assuming that you could earn an interest rate of 5 percent annually, you would need to build up investments of $1,400,000 ($1,400,000 x 5% = $70,000). With interest compounding at 5 percent, you would need to save $3,406 a month, or $40,872 a year, for 20 years to reach your goal. If you are at a higher income level, the news is worse. For example, if final household income is $120,000, according to the rule of thumb, you would need 70 percent of that, or $84,000. To achieve that amount, you would need a total of $1,680,000 in investments earning 5 percent per year. To get there, you would need to save $4,087 per month, or $49,044 a year, for 20 years.

That kind of saving isn't reasonable for most people, but don't panic. Remember: It's just a myth.

First of all, you probably won't need 70 percent of your pre-retirement income after you retire if you live within your means during your working years. That's because you won't have many of the expenses you had before, such as mortgage payments; child care; schooling costs; children's food, clothing, and entertainment costs; car-lease payments; and vacation costs for a family, to name a few.

The best way to analyze what you'll actually need isn't to use a simple percentage, but to assess where your money is going right now. Then you'll be able to clearly see if there are expenses you can reduce, and you'll certainly see what expenses may not even exist in your retirement years. So step one is calculating your expenses for the last year (if you have not already done so). If you don't do this, the whole process will be at risk. Just as any successful business keeps accurate and current financial records, you too need good information about your past spending habits in order to plan for your future. (Later on, in Chapter 11, you'll learn all you need to know about how to set up and track your finances.)

Let's look at an example that shows why the 70 percent myth is just that, and to give you some ideas for your own retirement planning. Meet the Hart family, who will serve throughout this book as one family's trek to successful financial and retirement planning. Your own financial affairs, of course, will be different, but you can use the story of the Harts as a touchstone for making your sound financial decisions.

Meet the Harts Today

Joe and Karen Hart are both 42 years old. They have two children: Colin, age 6, and Anita, who is 3. They live in a detached house in the suburbs.

Life is hectic for the Harts. Joe works as a computer software designer for a small company, and Karen is an accounting supervisor in a large law firm. Karen's mom looks after Anita during the weekdays, and Colin is in grade 1 at a public school near the house. Each weekday means a lot of travel time, as Joe takes Colin to school and goes on to work, and Karen drops Anita off at her mom's and goes to work.

Work life is also stressful. Joe's company is constantly on the hunt for venture capital, and there is a real possibility that he may lose his job if new investors can't be found.

Joe and Karen each make $50,000 for a combined income of $100,000, but after deductions for income tax, Employment Insurance (EI), Canada Pension Plan (CPP), and making RRSP contributions of $4,000 each (in Ontario, 2012), they're left with a net amount of $39,555 each. That's $79,110 for the family to cover all their expenses.

The Harts lease two automobiles: a Ford Taurus and a Honda Accord. With two kids and two jobs, they need both cars. They bought their house several years ago for $275,000; the mortgage at the beginning of the current year was $200,000, so they still are making substantial payments on it.

Now let's look at where the rest of the money went. The following spending record summarizes their outflows (i.e., all expenses plus any debt repayments and investments) for the year:

Expenses	$
Automobiles (2 leased cars)	14,756
Cash expenses	3,300
Children (daycare, lessons, babysitter)	3,900
Clothing	4,000
Entertainment (movie rentals, gifts, vacations)	4,650
Groceries	7,550
House (mortgage interest, property tax)	15,250
House repairs and maintenance	3,000
Insurance (house, car, life)	3,100
Interest and bank charges (bank, credit card)	2,100
Medical	1,600
Restaurants	2,980
Utilities (gas/oil, hydro, cable TV)	4,300
Total Expenses	**70,486**
Debt Repayment, Investments	
House mortgage principal	5,384
RRSPs	8,000
Total Debt Repayment, Investments	**13,384**
Total Outflows	**83,870**

You will have noticed that the Harts' outflow of $83,870 is greater than the $79,110 they bring home each year by $4,760. You may be wondering how this is possible. The Harts managed the same way many Canadians do; they used their credit cards and accumulated debt. In fact, they accumulated a debt of $4,760, charging 19 percent interest. On an annual basis, that will cost them $904 in interest – money that can never be recovered.

Of course, it is vital that the Harts get their spending under control before they entertain any thoughts of a comfortable retirement. They need to pay off their debts first; then they can start thinking about those years down the road. (Chapter 11 covers how to gain control over your expenses.)

The Harts after Retirement

Joe and Karen's situation will change considerably after they retire, and they project that their expenses will be reduced at that time. Here are the categories in which they expect to realize some savings:

• *Automobiles:* Joe and Karen probably won't need two cars, since they won't have two jobs to go to and won't be doing the "double kid shuffle." If they get rid of one of the cars – say the Honda – that will reduce their expenses by $6,885 per year, as that is what the leasing and operating costs came to last year. As for the other car, there will probably be a lot less mileage and wear, since there won't be daily trips to the office, school etc. They could also consider buying instead of leasing their car. (Chapter 10 discusses leasing versus buying in detail.) A well-maintained car should last eight to ten years, and possibly even longer. If the Harts purchase the car and pay it off before retirement, that will eventually lead to payment-free years, reducing car expenses by the leasing costs: $4,536 a year.

• *Cash expenses, children, clothing:* As with most families, a large portion of the cash in the Hart family is spent on the children. After retirement, those expenses will be gone because the kids will have grown up and left home. To be conservative, let's say only $1,000 of the $3,300 was spent on them. That's $1,000 less per year the couple will need after the kids move out. Direct children costs will also be eliminated, resulting in annual savings of $3,900. Clothing costs will also decline, let's say by $2,000 in this case.

• *Entertainment:* Let's assume entertainment expenses will not decline. With more free time the Harts expect to increase the number of movie rentals and vacations. The actual dollar amount will not increase, however, because the costs of the added rentals and trips will be lower than when they had to pay for the children travelling with them on vacation.

• *Groceries:* Grocery costs will also decline by an estimated $2,000 with half the number of mouths to feed.

• *House:* The current household mortgage is $200,000. It bears interest at 6 percent a year and is amortized over 20 years. The monthly payments are $1,424. After the mortgage has been eliminated, the Harts can cross off $17,092 from the outflows ($11,708 in interest and $5,384 in principal payments). Only the property taxes of $3,542 and repairs and maintenance of $3,000 will remain.

• *Insurance:* Insurance costs should decline when the Harts cut back to using one car. They may also decide to cancel the life insurance as they age since they will no longer have dependents relying on them financially. Insurance therefore declines by say $1,000.

• *Interest and bank charges:* These should decline as Joe and Karen are determined to pay off their credit card debt and stay away from costly bank overdraft protection interest charges. After retirement, only minimal bank charges should remain. That's another expense reduction of about $1,500 a year.

• *Medical, restaurants, and utilities:* The Harts assume that the total of medical costs, restaurant meals, and utilities will not decline.

• *RRSPs:* Joe and Karen will no longer be making RRSP contributions after retirement, which will result in lower cash outflows of $8,000 before tax.

Here's how today's expenses compare to post-retirement expenses:

Expenses	Current $	After Retirement $
Automobiles (2 leased cars)	14,756	3,335
Cash expenses	3,300	2,300
Children (daycare, lessons, babysitter)	3,900	0
Clothing	4,000	2,000
Entertainment (movie rentals, gifts, vacations)	4,650	4,650

Groceries	7,550	5,550
House (mortgage interest, property tax)	15,250	3,542
House repairs and maintenance	3,000	3,000
Insurance (house, car, life)	3,100	2,100
Interest and bank charges (bank, credit card)	2,100	600
Medical	1,600	1,600
Restaurants	2,980	2,980
Utilities (gas/oil, hydro, cable TV)	4,300	4,300
Total Expenses	**70,486**	**35,957**
Debt Repayment, Investments		
House mortgage principal	5,384	0
RRSPs	8,000	0
Total Debt Repayment, Investments	**13,384**	**0**
Total Outflows	**83,870**	**35,957**

To sum up, after Joe and Karen retire, they will reduce their cash outflows by an astounding $47,913 to $35,957, less than half what they are spending now.

This comparison of expenses reveals that the Harts will have to earn only approximately $40,000 per annum ($20,000 each) to net $35,957 after tax because they will both be in lower tax brackets and won't have CPP and EI withheld after they retire. In fact in 2012 they would net $18,252 each – $36,504 in total, which would leave them with a little more than they would need to meet their expenses. This amount is only 40 percent of their combined annual salary of $100,000 – far less than the 70 percent proposed by the myth supported by many financial advisors.

From Myth to Reality

So if the 70 percent myth isn't true, then how do you calculate how much you will need and where you'll get the money?

First, consider that you will have other sources besides the interest on your RRSP investments. So far, the calculations we've made are based on the assumption that you will live off investment interest and keep the principal to pass on to your children or other beneficiaries, which, perhaps, may be something you don't want – or need – to do. As you get older, you may feel comfortable relying on some of that principal for your daily expenses.

But even if you want to leave a significant portion of your RRSP investments intact, there are other sources of retirement income. These include the following:

• *Private pension plan:* If you've been one of the fortunate Canadians to have worked in a job that provides pension income, you should be able to rely on those payments.

• *Old Age Security (OAS):* The OAS pension is available to Canadian citizens and legal residents of Canada aged 65 and older who have lived in Canada for at least ten years since turning 18 years of age. Note that the age is gradually increasing to 67 over the next few years. As of the period July to September 2012, the maximum monthly OAS benefit was $544.98 ($6,540 yearly). If your individual net income is more than $69,562 you must repay part of your OAS pension. The repayment amounts are normally deducted from your monthly payments before they are issued. The full OAS pension is eliminated if your net income is $112,966 or more.

• *Canada Pension Plan (CPP):* If you pay into CPP during your working life, you are eligible for pension benefits as early as age 60. The maximum monthly CPP benefit payable for those at least 65 years old in 2012 was $986.67 per month or $11,840 annually.

Keep in mind that both OAS and CPP are adjusted for inflation. CPP is adjusted annually in January, and OAS is adjusted quarterly. These adjustments will, to a large degree, offset rising expenses. (For current rates for OAS and CPP, do an Internet search for "Income security rate card").

Now you can breathe a little easier knowing that you don't need 70 percent of your income for your retirement years. That is likely a relief – but you still need to determine what you will need. Let's revisit the Harts to see how their calculations are coming along.

The Harts: Making the Calculations

Joe and Karen have determined that they will need $40,000 per year in their retirement years. An advisor has told them that if they want to live solely off investment income, they will need to build up their investments to about $800,000, if they assume they can earn a 5 percent return

($800,000 x 5% = $40,000). That's a daunting figure for a couple that is already in debt and living a busy, stressful life.

If they were only relying on their RRSPs, Joe and Karen would need to have built them up to a combined value of $563,800 at retirement to generate annual RRSP payouts of $40,000 (at 5 percent for 25 years until they are 90 years old). The total, $563,800, is a lot less daunting to them than $800,000, the figure they started with, but it's still quite a bit of money.

The combined value of the couple's RRSPs is currently only $60,000. To build that up to $563,800 by age 65 (23 years) they would need to save $9,160 a year at a rate of return of 5 percent per annum, which is more than the $8,000 they are investing in RRSPs right now.

But there is more good news. Both Joe and Karen will be eligible for OAS when they turn 65, and they will not have to repay any of it, since their net incomes will be well below the "clawback" level. This means they can count on receiving $6,540 each, or $13,080, from the government every year. That reduces the amount that they will have to finance themselves from $40,000 to $26,920 ($40,000 less $13,080).

As well, because they both have paid into CPP all their working lives, they will be able to depend on those pension payments too. They determine that they will be eligible to receive the maximum monthly CPP benefit ($11,840 x 2 = $23,680), which will again reduce the amount they need to finance themselves. Now they need to find a way to come up with only $3,240 a year more ($40,000 less $13,080 OAS less $23,680 CPP).

The result? Joe and Karen realize that if they were to retire today they would only need an RRSP of $45,664 to provide $3,240 per year for 25 retirement years, assuming a 5 percent rate of return.

Things don't look so daunting now compared to their initial calculation, when they believed the 70 percent myth, which told them they would need $1,400,000. Is it any wonder Joe and Karen used to get depressed after a visit to their investment advisor?

The Effects of Inflation

You'll note that I have used the Harts' current salaries and expenses and have not attempted to project them to final pre-retirement levels. This is done to keep the example simple. As time goes by, it's important to continually update your own figures, since even small changes can have significant effects on the future. We'll get into this in detail in Chapter 3.

Inflation will surely have an effect. In the case of the Harts, if inflation averages say, 3 percent a year until they retire in 23 years, their $100,000 combined salaries would (hopefully!) rise to $197,360. Expenses will, of course, increase as well, but when those expenses are significantly reduced, so is the exposure to inflation.

The most common measure of inflation is the Consumer Price Index (CPI), which is the rate at which the price of a specific basket of goods rises each year. Because it is an average, it can be misleading. What is important to each of us is not some average figure, but the price of only what we buy as individuals. For example, if housing prices rise rapidly after you retire, it will only affect your expenses to the extent that your property taxes and repairs and maintenance increase if they are based on market value. The inflationary effect on your house value would be a good thing, since after you retire you are usually in the market to sell rather than buy.

The Harts' current expenses are $70,486. If inflation averages 3 percent over the next 23 years, they will go up to $139,110. But after retirement, the Harts calculate their expenses will be only $35,957 in today's dollars. In 23 years that figure will rise to only $70,964 assuming 3 percent inflation. At the same time, their salaries will have increased by $97,360 due to inflation. So in this situation of rising income and declining expenses, inflation actually works in the Harts' favour.

If the examples used in this chapter for the Harts were adjusted for inflation, you would see that the couple would be even better off. (We will deal with inflation in detail in Chapter 7.)

The Net Worth Statement

It's time to look at something that most people never see but which is an important piece of information in the quest for a financially secure retirement: the net worth statement. How it looks when you retire will go a long way to determining how comfortable your twilight years will be.

Your personal net worth statement is like a company's balance sheet. It shows the current value of all assets owned and liabilities owed at a point in time. It is different than your spending record, which is similar to a company's income statement and shows what amount of money came in and where it went over a period of time (usually a year).

After you stop working you won't have any employment income to pay your expenses. Unless you are scheduled for a great inheritance or win the lottery, the assets on your net worth statement at that time will be all that brings in money to pay your expenses (besides government and other pensions).

For most people, a house is their biggest asset. Owning a home is an excellent investment, especially if the mortgage is paid off. You have several options that can help you significantly. You could sell the home outright, pocket the proceeds tax-free, and buy a smaller house or a condominium. You could even move into a rental unit and make payments on a monthly basis. Alternatively, you could take out an equity line of credit. Any of these options would free up a significant amount of cash to handle emergencies or changes in circumstances. However, you also must be aware that you'll be eating into your net worth by adding debt, and that might not be too popular with your kids!

Your debts (liabilities) are just as important as your assets when you retire. Your cash outflows are going to be a lot higher if you still have debts. You'll need to have saved a lot more money before retirement to continue to make those payments.

Simply stated, your objective should be to maximize the value of your assets and eliminate all debts by the time you retire. If you have a current statement of net worth looking you in the face every year, it'll be much easier to ensure you are on the right track to making it the best it can be by the time you retire.

Now let's consider Joe and Karen's statement of net worth.

The Harts' Net Worth

Here is Joe and Karen Harts' statement of net worth at the end of this year, compared to the end of last year:

David Trahair

	December 31, Last year $	December 31, This year $
Assets		
Cash in bank	714	714
House (principal residence)	275,000	275,000
RRSPs (combined market value)	53,775	60,000
Total assets	**329,489**	**335,714**
Liabilities		
House mortgage	200,000	194,616
Credit card balance	0	4,760
Total liabilities	**200,000**	**199,376**
Net Worth (assets – liabilities)	**129,489**	**136,338**

As you can see, they are in pretty good financial shape with a net worth of $136,338, which is better than last year by $6,849.

Even though they invested $8,000 in RRSPs this year and paid down the principal on their mortgage by $5,384, their net worth did not increase by the total of that investment plus debt principal repayments ($13,384). Why not? There are several reasons.

First of all, their RRSPs did not do so well, rising by only $6,225 ($60,000 – $53,775) even though they contributed $8,000. They in fact had a return this past year of -2.8 percent.

Second, as already mentioned, they spent $4,760 more than they made in the current year. The effect of their overspending has a significant effect on their net worth statement. At the end of this year, they still had $714 in the bank but owed $4,760 on the credit card – the exact amount by which they overspent.

If Joe and Karen pay off their credit card balance and get back to putting $8,000 per year into their RRSPs, their combined value will grow to $515,700 in 23 years at 5 percent. That amount is significantly more than the minimum RRSP value of $45,664 that we previously calculated. This excess amount will go a long way to covering many of the uncertainties they are sure to face.

You may notice that there are some things missing from the net worth statement. Joe and Karen own personal property, including furniture, clothing, and electronic equipment, that is not listed. These types of items, while they have value, do not really contribute to the couple's ability to retire. This exercise is meant to analyze the couple's net worth with the objective of maximizing the amount of money they have and optimizing its structure to ensure that they can reach their retirement goals.

Summary

It should be clear by now that if you get your finances under control and retire debt-free you could get by fine on much less than 70 percent of your current income after you retire. In the case of the Harts, they've learned that they could get by on less than half of the money they make now and that they could get there without contributing anything more to their RRSPs if they get their spending under control and pay off all debts. Your case will most certainly be different. You may need more or maybe less.

If you have done your own calculations and determined that you'll only need half of what you make now, does that mean you no longer need to invest or be concerned about your future? Of course not.

After you pay off all your debts, you want to put away as much as you can for the future as a cushion against events such as rising medical expenses or simply as a supplement to your travel fund.

Read on to learn more ways to do so – ways that are probably not in accordance with what you've heard from your financial advisor.

3. Myth 2: RRSPs Are the Holy Grail of Retirement

Exposing the Myth

If you are like most Canadians, when someone asks you about your retirement plans, you probably start talking about your Registered Retirement Savings Plan (RRSP). That's because most Canadians don't have a gold-plated company pension plan to rely on.

But RRSPs are not the Holy Grail of retirement planning, and you want to be careful before jumping into the yearly sales pitches that pressure you to invest the maximum allowed. This doesn't mean RRSPs should be avoided. Used wisely, they can be a significant part of a secure retirement. The problem is that most people focus only on their RRSPs and forget the other parts that are even more important – their spending patterns and debt levels.

The main benefit of an RRSP is tax-related. You get a tax refund right away and the investments grow within your RRSP on a tax-free basis until you withdraw the money. That's a real economic gain because of the time value of money – you can use the tax refund now and have to pay it back only when you retire. If your RRSP investments rise, they can produce a great nest egg and save you money in the process. And that's why I do recommend that you start investing in RRSPs effectively – but only after you pay off all your personal debt, including your house mortgage.

The Warm Bath

Think about retirement as a nice warm bath. You're busting your buns your whole working life to fill that bathtub with soothing hot water so you can soak your aching bones after work. But what's the most efficient way to do it? Most people get advice on how to fill their bathtub from a bathwater salesperson. What is this person going to tell you? They'll most likely look into your tub and give a thoughtful, "Hmmm..." and say, "Gee, there's not much water in there. You should have started filling it much earlier. You're going to have to put a lot more in from now on if you want to have any hope of filling this bathtub! Oh, and by the way, we can help you."

But there's something important that the salesperson doesn't bother to tell you – the plug is missing! That's right: Water-and in the case of personal finances, money, is flowing down the drain every second of every day as you are trying to fill up your tub.

Here's the key: put the plug in and then start filling! Let's bring the analogy back to finances. Have you ever heard a similar pitch from a mutual fund salesperson?

Don't listen. Instead, take control.

An RRSP Primer

Let's review the basics before discussing when and how you should begin investing more of your hard-earned money in an RRSP. (We'll deal extensively with how much to put in your RRSP in Chapter 7.)

An RRSP is not simply an investment. It is a government-sanctioned registered program that allows you to save for your retirement. You are allowed to invest in a broad range of products within an RRSP, including GICs, mutual funds, individual stocks, and bonds. There are strict rules on how much you are allowed to invest.

RRSP Limits

Your RRSP limit for the current year is determined as follows:
- Your unused RRSP deduction limit carried forward from prior years, plus:
- 18 percent of your previous year's earned income (up to a maximum of $22,970 in 2012 and $23,820 in 2013), less:
- Any pension adjustment for the prior year (for those who have company pension plans).

(Note: Earned income includes salary, wages, and self-employment income but not investment income.)

Foreign Content

Until several years ago, you were allowed to hold up to 30 percent of your RRSP in foreign investments based on their "book value" (i.e., the cost of the investment plus any mutual fund distributions). For example, if you invested $10,000 in your RRSP and put $7,000 in a Canadian GIC, you could invest up to $3,000 in a foreign mutual fund. Even if the foreign investment rose in value to, say, $4,000, and your Canadian content stayed at $7,000, you were still all right. That is why your RRSP statement used to show you the book value – to make sure you stayed within the foreign content limits.

The foreign content limit was removed in January 2005. Your RRSP statement therefore no longer has to show book value, even though it is very useful in determining how well your RRSP investments are doing. This provides a golden opportunity for you to see how your RRSP company reacted. Did it eliminate book value from your statements or did they keep showing it so you can make informed decisions about your investments? Look at your new statements – is your company trying to keep you informed or are they playing the usual games?

Timing

For an RRSP contribution to be deductible, it must be made within 60 days of the calendar year-end (i.e., March 1, or February 29 in a leap year). If the deadline falls on a weekend, it is extended to the next business day.

Debunking the Promises of RRSPs

The mythology of the power of RRSPs is really an accumulation of several claims that have built up over time. Let's look at each in turn.

Start Yesterday

Here's the claim: If you want to retire in comfort, you have to put money into your RRSP every year, and it's best to start when you are young. The younger the better. If you start an RRSP when you are just 22 years old and you put $4,000 in per year until you are 65 at an annual rate of return of 8 percent, your RRSP will be worth $1.3 million when you retire!

I am tired of hearing this pitch because it's really nothing more than a slick marketing trick that can be lethal to your financial health. There are many problems with it.

First, consider who is sending the message. It's all the usual suspects: banks, brokerage houses, and many "financial advisors." Why do they want you to fall for this message? Because for every dollar you put in, they get a percentage. It's a guaranteed annuity for them, regardless of what happens to your investments along the way.

When you hand over your money to your advisor or banker to invest in an RRSP, he or she will invest it for you. If he or she invests in a mutual fund, in addition to any upfront commission, he or she will also get an annual fee from the mutual fund company. You will never know how much your advisor or banker is getting, however, because this cost is buried in the expenses of the mutual fund company. This cost is included in the management expense ratio, or MER. It represents the ratio of costs, including commissions and marketing expenses, as a percentage of the total assets of the mutual fund. All investors in that fund are paying those management expenses, and it can all add up to a lot of money.

For example, say the managers of the mutual fund were able to realize a return on their investments of 7 percent. If the MER is 2 percent, the overall rate of return on that mutual fund would be only the net amount of 5 percent. The theory is that the managers are being rewarded for generating above-average returns. That's fine if they do, but in many cases they don't. Your broker and the mutual fund company win. You lose.

The second problem with this claim is that it ignores some basic facts of life. Where is the typical 22-year-old going to come up with $4,000 per year? He or she has possibly just graduated from university and perhaps has a student loan. As with any debt, that loan will have a fixed interest rate that in many cases will exceed what can be earned in the RRSP. (See Chapter 4 for more information.) Nor should a 22-year-old borrow the money to invest in an RRSP. Increasing debt at this age is the last thing anyone should be considering.

In addition, no one is even allowed to invest in an RRSP until he or she has a job or other earned income to create RRSP contribution room.

Lastly, does it really make sense for a 22-year-old to be worried about retirement? In every stage of life, you need to set your priorities both personally and financially. What about seeing the world and enjoying some life experiences before settling down to marriage, kids, a home, and all the rest? Frankly, I don't think focusing on retirement from the day he or she gets out of school is the best advice to give a young adult!

27

David Trahair

Borrow if You Don't Have the Funds

"Don't have the cash for an RRSP contribution? No problem. We'll lend you the money!"

You can hear that offer every February. Here's why you shouldn't listen to it.

Borrowing to invest makes sense in the long term only if the rate of return exceeds the interest rate on the loan. Obviously, it doesn't make sense to borrow at 5 percent to invest in a term deposit making only 2 percent! If you do borrow to invest, you are essentially agreeing to put all your eggs in one basket – the stock market – and hoping that it beats the rate on your loan. Once again, this strategy plays directly into the hands of those people who make a living off your finances.

Invest in an RRSP before Paying Down the Mortgage

This question of whether or not it's wise to invest in an RRSP before paying off the mortgage also comes up every year. The usual answer is that you should contribute the maximum to your RRSP and use the tax refund to pay down your mortgage. Sounds like a good compromise doesn't it? This way, the finance company gets your investment money and it's up to you to be disciplined enough to actually use the refund to pay down your mortgage. Of course, that's easier said than done.

First of all, you need to be able to afford to pay down your mortgage. In other words, you mustn't need the refund for anything else, such as paying down other debt or taking a much-needed vacation. Second, usually you can only pay down a mortgage when the finance company allows you to. Often that's only once a year and is limited to 15 percent to 20 percent of the outstanding balance. You have to be very disciplined and make sure you put the refund into a safe place until then.

The reality is that investing in an RRSP and using the tax refund to pay down the mortgage is usually not a compromise at all. The people who send this message are, in fact, simply getting you to invest in an RRSP. Period. I am saying pay down the mortgage instead. Period.

Another Problem with RRSPs

What happens if you are heavily invested in stocks when you are about to retire? What about the thousands of other baby boomers in the same situation? Lots of Canadians are going to be forced to sell their stocks and mutual funds to fund their retirements. Some will start earlier, and some will be able to afford to delay withdrawing money until age 71, when they must begin making the minimum RRIF withdrawals. What will that do to the stock market? No one knows for sure, but if more people are selling than buying, its most likely direction is down.

This will be happening at the worst time possible – when there is little time left to correct it and when no employment income can be earned to replace it. You may want to consider reducing your exposure to this risk, and that means reducing your investments in stocks and equity mutual funds.

Another Day Older and Deeper in Debt?

If you focus all your resources and efforts on your RRSP and not on eliminating your debts, you'll probably still be left with those mortgage payments, car loan, or lease payments, and maybe even credit card balances when you retire. I have said it before, but it bears repeating: you will need to save a lot more money for retirement if you have to continue making all those payments.

From the bank or finance company's point of view, of course, your being in debt at retirement is ideal. Think about it. They get commissions and fees on all your RRSP contributions from the time you start to invest until you retire. They lock you into as much debt as possible: a mortgage, car loans or lease payments, credit card debt, and perhaps a home equity line of credit for good measure. You continue paying them even after you retire. That way, they'll also "work the spread" and make money off the deposits from other people who are funding your loans. They are winning on both sides of the balance sheet – investments from you and loans to you – who is losing? You guessed it: you are.

David Trahair

Debt: The Good, the Bad, and the Ugly

In Canada today, only the fortunate few can afford to pay cash for big-ticket items such as houses and cars. The rest of us must finance these purchases or we'd never get to own them. Mortgages and car loans are examples of good debt. It is necessary for us to take on this kind of debt to begin enjoying the assets, with an added bonus for houses – the value of that particular asset generally increases over time. The other advantage is one of cash flow. After the house and car are paid off, you will require less cash to live each year, and that ties into the idea of optimizing your RRSP, as we'll soon discuss.

Bad debt, on the other hand, includes lines of credit used to finance things such as vacations and luxury items like TVs and electronic gadgets. While the things we purchase this way may make us feel good, they are coming at a price – interest. Waiting until you have earned the cash to buy the things will save you a lot.

Ugly debt? Think credit cards and interest on personal income taxes owing from prior years.

An Alternative Strategy

Now for a radical thought. If paying off all personal debt before you retire is a good idea, why not focus on paying it all off even sooner? Why not forget RRSP contributions altogether until you pay off all debt, including your house mortgage?

Consider the rate of return on your debt with this strategy. For example, suppose you have a house mortgage at 6 percent, a car loan at 8 percent, and a credit card balance at 19 percent. Simply by paying off your debts instead of investing in an RRSP, you can realize a guaranteed after-tax return of between 6 and 19 percent, and there is no risk related to this rate of return.

Now let's consider this strategy in the case of Joe and Karen Hart.

The Harts: Investing in RRSPs Versus Paying Down the Debt

If Joe and Karen continue to spend more than they make, any financial strategy will almost certainly be doomed to failure. But they are determined to get their spending under control, and want to know, therefore, whether they will do better by investing $8,000 a year ($4,000 each) in RRSPs (see Chart 1: RRSP Option) or paying down their mortgage by $8,000 a year (see Chart 2: Mortgage Pay- Down Option).

They begin their calculations as of December 31 of last year, when they had no credit card debt, and make the following assumptions:

- The RRSPs will grow at an average rate of 5 percent per year.
- The mortgage rate will remain at 6 percent annually.
- Their marginal personal tax rates are 31 percent.
- The tax savings on the RRSP contributions will be re- invested in those RRSPs (i.e., they have sufficient contribution room).

Note that we will only look at the effect on net worth of two lines on the Harts' net worth statement: total RRSP value and mortgage balance. We are assuming the other lines (cash in bank, house value, etc.) will be the same for both scenarios. Here is a comparison of the two scenarios after 1, 5, 11, and 20 years:

CHART 1 – RRSP OPTION – $8,000 per year contributed to RRSPs

	31-Dec Last Year	31-Dec Year 1	31-Dec Year 5	31-Dec Year 11	31-Dec Year 20
Assets					
RRSPs (combined market value)	$53,775	$66,956	$126,607	$241,031	$489,609
Liabilities					
House mortgage	$200,000	$194,660	$169,799	$119,348	$0
Net Worth Effect (assets – liabilities)	-$146,225	-$127,704	-$43,192	$121,683	$489,609

David Trahair

CHART 2 – RRSP OPTION – $8,000 per year towards mortgage pay-down

	31-Dec Last Year	31-Dec Year 1	31-Dec Year 5	31-Dec Year 11	31-Dec Year 20
Assets					
RRSPs (combined market value)	$53,775	$56,464	$68,832	$91,974	$507,025
Liabilities					
House mortgage	$200,000	$186,437	$123,286	$0	$0
Net Worth Effect (assets – liabilities)	-$146,225	-$129,973	-$54,654	$91,974	$507,025

The results after one year are very close. The RRSP option shows -$127,704, while the mortgage pay-down option shows a -$129,973 effect on net worth. Even after five years, the RRSP option beats the mortgage pay-down option by $11,462 (difference between -$43,192 and -$54,654).

After 11 years, the RRSP option is still ahead by $29,709 ($121,683 less $91,974), but there is an important factor to consider – income tax.

The RRSP option shows a higher RRSP value, but to access those funds, the Harts would have to pay taxes on any withdrawal. To pay off the mortgage after 11 years, they would have to cash in $198,000 of their RRSPs to be left with the required $119,348. That's $99,000 from each RRSP, less the $39,326 in tax they each would have to pay if it was added to their $50,000 salaries. They would be left with the required $59,674 each ($119,348 in total). That would leave them with only $43,031 in RRSPs, versus $91,974 for the mortgage pay-down scenario. The higher amount of net worth is deceptive because a large portion of it is pre-tax.

With the debt pay-down strategy, the Harts' mortgage will be paid off in 11 years (in fact, in ten years and seven months). That will leave them with more than nine mortgage-free years. During those last nine years, they will have an extra $1,424 per month to invest. That's the money that will no longer be going to the mortgage, and it adds up to more than $17,000 a year. Now they can begin to focus on their RRSPs in earnest.

After 20 years, the debt pay-down scenario shows a net worth slightly higher than for the RRSP scenario – a difference of $17,416 ($507,025 less $489,609). So after 20 years, the Harts would arrive at a similar point but would have taken a very different journey. The debt pay- down scenario, however, has two major advantages: it reduces the risk that the Harts could lose their house during the nine years of mortgage-free living, and there is less risk related to investment returns.

How much confidence do you have that the markets are going to post better returns than the interest rate on your debt? Are you willing to stake your family's future on it?

The Burden of Debt

Think of debt as a ball and chain attached to your ankle. That's what is holding you back in the race for financial freedom – not the fact that you didn't start contributing to an RRSP when you were a kid or that you haven't been able to max out your contributions.

In looking at the continuing story of the Harts, we see a family that is in good financial shape. The only debt they have is their mortgage. But what about people who aren't in such a strong financial position? If the debt pay-down option beats the RRSP when dealing with only a mortgage at 6 percent, think about those people with credit card debt at 19 percent or higher.

Credit Card Debt

Credit card debt is probably the most common debt for many Canadians. Anyone with credit card debt should pay it off first before making another RRSP contribution. You simply can't beat the rate of return. Let's look at an example.

Billy has $10,000 owing on his super-deluxe gold credit card. He is being charged 19 percent a year for his past indulgences. He is in the 40 percent tax bracket and therefore would receive a 40 percent tax refund on an RRSP contribution. He also has an extra $300 per month available.

This is what Billy discovers when he runs the figures through a simple spreadsheet program to compare paying down debt to making RRSP contributions:

- Billy would have to make monthly payments of $259.41 to pay off his credit card in five years (60 months). If he puts his extra $300 per month into his RRSP and re-invests the tax refund into the same RRSP, he will have paid off the credit card and have a balance of $28,358 in his RRSP at the end of five years.
- If instead of putting the $300 a month into an RRSP, Billy adds it to his regular credit card payments, he would have the debt cleared in just over 21 months. He could then start investing $559.41 a month in his RRSP (the $259.41 he would still be paying under the RRSP option plus the $300). At the end of five years, his RRSP would be worth $32,699. That's $4,341 better off.

It bears repeating: pay off credit card debt first!

Income Tax Debt

If you owe personal taxes from prior years, the debt is attracting interest at the "prescribed rate" set by the government (5 percent, in the third quarter of 2012), and it's not tax deductible.

Tax debt isn't like credit card debt, which you can take decades to pay off, if you wish. The government wants its money and it wants it soon. They also have the power to collect the money by contacting your bank directly and demanding payment, freezing your bank account, garnishing your wages, possessing your assets, etc. In short, it can get ugly.

If you have this kind of debt, you don't want it hanging around. If you owe on your taxes, focus on paying that first – even before credit card debt.

The Joys of Debt-Free Living

Stop for a minute and think about what it would be like not to have any debt at all – no credit card debt, nothing owing on the car, not even mortgage payments. There would be no pressure to bring in a salary to make the payments. If you were to lose your job or become disabled and lose your ability to work, you wouldn't be in danger of losing your house.

Free Disability Insurance

Paying off the mortgage is like providing your own disability or income protection insurance. That is because if you don't owe any money on your mortgage and you lose the ability to earn income, you won't have to replace the income that previously went to pay the mortgage.

Statistically the odds of becoming disabled are much higher than the odds of dying, yet many people are more likely to have life insurance than disability insurance. The costs associated with becoming disabled are also very high: not only will you have regular living costs, there also may be the costs of ongoing attendant care, medicine, and other charges. If you can't continue to earn income, you could be in trouble. If your house is paid for, your worries will be significantly reduced.

Using Your House for Emergency Funds

You may have heard of the rule of thumb that you should save up about three months of expenses, just in case you need extra money in times of an emergency. But if you've been trying to pay off debt and invest in RRSPs, where is that money going to come from?

At first glance, you might think that your RRSPs would provide a great fund to draw on in times of emergency. But you must remember: an RRSP is designed as a long-term savings vehicle, not as a temporary emergency fund. Here's why:

- First, if you withdraw funds from your RRSP, you will have to pay income tax on the withdrawal, which can be significant, depending on your tax bracket. The amount withdrawn will be taxed based on your income level and in which province you live. If you withdraw $10,000 out of an RRSP, and you're taxed at 37 percent, for example, you'll receive only $6,300.
- Second, if you need to access your RRSP funds at a time when your investments are down in the stock market, you will be forced to realize your paper losses. If you have invested

$10,000 in RRSPs, but the stock market has declined, your $10,000 may be worth only, say, $8,000 when you need to access it. If you need the funds, you'll have to sell them at $8,000, eliminating any hope that they could rise in value again in the future.

- Finally, if your RRSPs are invested in mutual funds, you need to consider any deferred sales charges (DSC). In many cases, you will pay a fee up to 6 percent in the first year to cash in your funds. The DSC fee usually does not decline to zero until you have held the mutual fund for six years.

With the debt pay-down strategy, you may not have an emergency fund, but you will have something just as good – an equity interest in your house. That means if you find yourself needing money, you could tap into that equity and take out a secured line of credit. If your finances are in order, a credit check won't be a problem for you. In fact, if you pay everything off, there won't be any credit to check!

A Word about RESPs and Group RRSPs

Registered Education Savings Plans (RESPs) allow you to invest money to pay for a child's post-secondary education. The contributions are not tax-deductible, but the investment income is allowed to grow in the plan on a tax-deferred basis. When the money is withdrawn to pay the tuition fees, the original contribution is returned tax-free (since the original contributions were not deducted) and any income earned in the plan is generally taxed in the hands of the child that attends the post-secondary school.

Since 2007 there has been no annual limit for contributions to RESPs and the lifetime limit is $50,000 per beneficiary. What makes RESPs so attractive, however, is the Canada Education Savings Grant (CESG). Under this plan, the federal government provides grants of up to 20 percent of annual contributions made to RESPs for beneficiaries up to and including age 17, to a maximum grant of $500 per year per beneficiary to a lifetime limit of $7,200.

For example, if you put $2,500 into an RESP for your child, the government will pay a grant of $500 to the RESP. That's like getting an immediate 20 percent return on your investment, and rivals the rate on many credit cards. There are now also additional CESG grants available that could increase the tax grant to 30 percent and even 40 percent on the first $500 depending on family income. For current details do an Internet search for "CESG limits." If you decide to put money into an RESP instead of paying down debt, it's vital that you carefully monitor the fees and rate of return that the RESP is generating.

Another possible exception to the debt pay-down strategy is group RRSPs. Some employers who don't have a traditional company pension plan offer this type of saving vehicle; they match, up to a certain maximum, any RRSP contribution that the employee makes. Say they allow you to contribute 3 percent of your salary of $50,000. That's $1,500 from you and they match it with another $1,500 to your plan. The 3 percent is free money that's difficult to turn down, but you must still remember to keep a close eye on the plan to make sure the returns are adequate and the fees are reasonable.

Summary

Add up your monthly debt payments now. Think about what it would be like not to have to make any of those payments. You'd have a lot left each month to invest, and you'd have no risk of losing your house, your car, or getting in over your head on credit cards if you lost your job. Since you wouldn't owe anything to anyone, there would be no one who could take things away from you.

Think about the effect of paying down debt on your net worth. A reduction in your debt is the same as an increase in your assets. In fact, a reduction in personal debt is better than an increase in an RRSP, because to get at the RRSP, you would need to pay tax on the withdrawal. The value of your RRSP when you retire is only one line on your net worth statement. What's on the other lines can be far more significant in determining your level of comfort.

The key to planning for a stress-free, enjoyable retirement can be summed up simply: pay off all your personal debt first, and then begin investing in RRSPs.

4. Myth 3: Don't Worry about Your Investments; You'll Be Fine in the Long Run

Exposing the Myth

For many years, the mantra of the financial community has been that if you want to have any hope of retiring in good shape, it is imperative to put your trust in the stock market. Don't worry about the conflict of interest between the analysts and the investment bankers that work for the same brokerage firm. Put your trust in the CEOs running the big companies – they're working hard for you and wouldn't put their own agenda ahead of shareholders like you. The stock market will recover: it always has in the past. Don't miss out!

Is investing the majority of your money in the stock market really the way to go? I, for one, am no longer convinced. Let's look at some of the factors to consider.

The Devastating Stock Market Crash

We have just lived through one of the most devastating stock market meltdowns since the Great Depression. Not too many people predicted it but we all knew it could happen, right?

Let's take a look at what happened. The S&P TSX Composite Index peaked on June 18, 2008 at 15,073. Over the next nine months, it declined and reached its pit on March 6, 2009 at 7,591. That is a decline of 49.6 percent – almost half its value.

It has since rebounded. By June 30, 2012, it had bounced back to 11,597. Here's where it gets interesting.

"That's a recovery of 52.8 percent!" we hear the industry yell. So we lost 49.6 percent but have now recovered 52.8 percent. Sounds pretty good, doesn't it? Well, it's not. They are fooling us with math. The problem with percentages is that they can be deceiving. Let me explain.

The key is the base you are starting with. Before the crash the base was the peak of 15,073. The index lost 7,482 points when it reached the bottom (15,073 − 7,591 = 7,482). The loss of 7,482 is 49.6 percent of 15,073 (7,482/15,073 = 49.6 percent). But now they start using the smaller base – the value on March 6, 2009 of 7,591. The index rose to 11,597 for a gain of 4,006 (11,597 – 7,591 = 4,006). That gain of 4,006 is 52.8 percent of 7,591 (4,006/7,591 = 52.8 percent).

But 4,006 points is only 26.6 percent of the original base at the peak – 15,073. We are still down 23 percent from the peak after the recovery (a loss of 49.6 percent less a recovery of 26.6 percent equals a loss of 23 percent).

Let's look at it using the original base of 15,073. The index has declined to 11,597 as of June 30, 2012. That's a loss of 3,476 points (15,073 – 11,597 = 3,476). That is 23 percent of 15,073 (3,476/15,073 = 23 percent).

Don't be fooled by percentages. If you had started with $15,073 invested in this index on June 18, 2008 you would only have had $11,597 on June 30, 2012. That hurts.

Long Term Rates

But this has been an atypical few years. What about the long term? We often hear that over the long term you can expect to make about 8 to 10 percent a year in the stock market. Is that true? Let's take a look.

First of all, what is long term? It depends. For a 25-year-old who plans to retire at 65, it's about 40 years. For a 55-year-old, it's only about 10 years until they'll need to start accessing the funds. We need to look at a number of different periods.

Look at the following table. I've calculated the average annual rate of return of the S&P TSX Composite Index for the last 10, 20, 30, 40, and 50 years to the peak of 15,073 on June 18, 2008.

BEFORE THE CRASH: Index value at June 18, 2008 of 15,073.

Years	10	20	30	40	50
Start month	Jun-98	Jun-88	Jun-78	Jun-68	Jun-58
Index value start	7,367	3.441	1,126	925	485
Average annual rate of return	7.42%	7.67%	9.03%	7.23%	7.11%

As you can see, the index did not quite reach the 8 to 10 percent return over any of the periods except over the last 30 or so years. But the returns are still quite good.

David Trahair

What about after the crash? The following table shows the average annual rates of return up to June 30, 2012.

AFTER THE CRASH: Index value at June 30, 2012 of 11,597

Years	10	20	30	40	50
Start month	Jun-02	Jun-92	Jun-82	Jun-72	Jun-62
Index value start	7,146	3,388	1,367	1,104	572
Average annual rate of return	**4.96%**	**6.35%**	**7.39%**	**6.06%**	**6.20%**

Interesting: The highest it got was 7.39 percent, again over the last 30 years. That is very close to the 8 to 10 percent assumption. But the real issue is how well you have done with your investments – not what the index has done.

How Mutual Funds Eat Your Money

Most Canadians invest in mutual funds to try to tap into potentially good stock market returns. They sure sound like a great idea. You get professional money managers to make sure you are adequately diversified, and they charge only a nominal fee. Mutual funds used to work well when returns were good, but what's happened lately? With lower returns available in the stock market, most mutual funds haven't been doing too well for us. Unluckily for the mutual fund managers, that has put a spotlight on the fees they are charging us. Guess what? They aren't so nominal.

Let's look at how many of them drain away our money, without us even realizing it. What does your mutual fund really cost you? It costs you about 2.5 percent per year for an average Canadian equity mutual fund through the management expense ratio, including an annual "trailer fee" to your advisor of somewhere around 0.5 percent every year you leave the money in the mutual fund, as I mentioned in the previous chapter. But there is another charge lurking.

The other significant fee is the cost to sell the mutual fund. Most Canadians don't want to pay an up-front commission to the broker, so they select a "deferred sales charge" (DSC) mutual fund. With a DSC mutual fund, the penalty for not paying an up-front commission is that you are often locked in for up to six or seven years! What if the fund doesn't perform well, and you want to sell it? You'll pay a commission as high as 6 percent in the first year. That commission declines each year but doesn't reach zero until the locked-in period expires.

Why doesn't everyone just buy stocks then? Because putting all your eggs in one basket is extremely risky. With retirement at stake, most of us cannot afford a major mistake.

Timing Is Everything

Analyzing the rate of return in the stock market is a pretty tough thing to do. Because of its volatility, the timing of the measurement can lead to some pretty bizarre results.

Consider the euphoria leading up to the crash of 2000. The average yearly rate of return from July 1990 to July 2000 on the S&P/TSX was 11.32 percent. But the reason the 10-year average looks so good is because of one great year. During the year ending July 2000, the index increased 45.5 percent. The next year, it declined by 26 percent.

Doing the calculation over a period of many years gives the false impression that the returns are consistent. Absolutely nothing could be further from the truth. If you look at the returns of any stock market, you'll see a similar trait. They are often up and down like a yoyo from one year to the next. There seems to be no logic to them. This situation allows the investment companies to play a game with us.

When the markets were booming, rate of return information was all over the place. Ads for mutual funds tout detailed information: one-year, two-year, five-year, ten-year returns. Look how great our managers are! Why don't you see these ads during a bear market? Because it wouldn't be good for their business.

When is the right time to get into the market? Obviously when the market is at a low point rather than a peak. However, most people tend to buy when everyone else is getting "rich" overnight. Who can resist when you hear that someone without investing experience made more than his or her annual salary in the market the previous year?

Assuming you want to get into the market, which month is best? October is one of the riskiest months to invest. The others are January to September, November and December!

David Trahair

Will the Future Be Like the Past?

The common thinking is that the stock market will rebound because it always has. But the question is, how long will it take?

What if returns over the next 10 to 20 years don't reach the historical rates of the past? What will happen if there is a bear market for that period of time, and you generate only a 3 percent return per year on average, even with the risk? Anyone who puts all his or her eggs in the RRSP investment basket will be in for a very tough ride.

Alternatives to Mutual Funds

There is no easy answer to how to invest. Some of us will never feel comfortable making our own investment decisions. For others, education is the key to gaining the confidence to take control of their investments. Spend time researching alternatives such as exchange-traded index funds. These are investments like stocks and they are listed on the stock exchanges. They simply invest in the companies that the major indexes do. They do have management expenses, but they are not mutual funds, and as a result, the expenses are much lower.

Don't like stocks at all? Spend time investigating the fixed income market – GICs, term deposits, bonds, etc. Here's something to get you started: The average five-year GIC interest rate from 2001 to 2010 was 3.6 percent. With interest rates at historical lows, it's not surprising they seem to be heading up. If you could lock in an average rate of return between now and your retirement at rates averaging, say, 5 percent, with no risk and no fees, would you?

The answer to the question "What should I invest in?" will depend on many factors: your aversion to risk, your age, inflation data, etc. The best answer for most people is probably a mix of low-cost equities and fixed income investments. The only thing that's certain is that the more you educate yourself about the options, the better off you'll be.

Your Personal Rate of Return

What Those Investment Statements Don't Tell You

It has always bewildered me why most investment companies send monthly statements that focus on the short term. What is the point of showing what the market value of your investments was last month and what it is this month? The focus should be on the long term. After all, you are investing for your retirement, and what's longer than that?

What they should tell you, but don't, is the annual rate of return on your portfolio for periods including year-to-date, the last year, and since you opened the account. You should also be provided with benchmark rates of returns for different investment types, both domestically and internationally, so you can determine how you are doing in relative terms. Additionally, you should be informed of the original cost of your investments so you can compare it to the current market value to see how many dollars you have gained or lost on each investment.

The problem is that the investment companies really don't want you to know this information, because your actual results may not be as rosy as those published numbers for the funds in which you may have some money invested. In most cases, you won't find any cost figures on your non-RRSP accounts, because they aren't forced to provide it.

Even if you have an unusual investment company that does provide some rate of return information, you may not be getting the whole story if you have more than one brokerage account. You need information on your investments as a whole, not just on one account. The big picture is what's important. For example, say you have two accounts with one broker, a discount brokerage account with someone else, and your spouse has one account at a third broker. Even if one or two of those investment companies provide rate of return information, you won't get the rate of return on all the investments put together. That's the most important one: your own personal rate of return.

Who's going to calculate that figure? You are, and I'll show how to do it right now.

43

David Trahair

Your Rate of Return Calculator

I have written a simple Microsoft Excel program called the Personal Rate of Return (PRR) calculator that you can download for free from my website at www.trahair.com. All you need are the dollar amounts and dates you invested, and the current market value. It's as simple as that. You don't need to concern yourself with stock splits, dividend re-investments, or mutual fund disbursements to compute your effective annual rate of return.

Let's look at an example. Suppose you diligently started making RRSP contributions ten years ago. Some years you put in more, and sometimes, when cash was tight, you put in less. Some years you left your contribution until the last day, and other times you didn't. You have several different broker accounts, some in stocks and others in various mutual funds with different commission load structures.

You enter all the contribution amounts and dates in the spreadsheet. The best way to get this information is to call your investment firms to see if they will provide you with a summary of contributions and withdrawals. Alternatively you can go through your old tax returns.

Figure 1
CALCULATING YOUR PERSONAL RATE OF RETURN

	A	B	C	D	E
1	THE PERSONAL RATE OF RETURN CALCULATOR				
2	Version 71112				
3					
4	Instructions:				
5	You must start on line 15 below by entering the first amount invested as a negative number in cell C15 with that date in cell B15.				
6	Remember to input contributions as negative numbers and withdrawals as positive numbers.				
7	All investments and withdrawals after that must be entered in date order from oldest to newest on subsequent lines.				
8	Insert more lines as needed between the initial amount invested and the current market value.				
9	Input the current market value as a positive number and date on the last line as if you sold the portfolio for that amount.				
10					
11					
12			Date	Amount	
13			contributed	Contributed	
14					
15	Enter initial amount invested here --->		2001-02-28	-$3,500.00	
16			2002-02-28	-$5,500.00	
17			2003-02-28	-$7,500.00	
18			2004-06-30	-$1,000.00	
19			2005-02-28	-$10,000.00	
20			2006-02-28	-$7,500.00	
21			2007-01-01	-$9,700.00	
22			2008-02-28	-$18,000.00	
23			2009-02-28	-$2,000.00	
24			2010-02-28	-$13,500.00	
25			2011-02-28	-$16,400.00	
26	Enter current market value and date here --->		2012-12-31	$100,000.00	
27					
28	Amount by which proceeds exceed contributions			$5,400.00	
29					
30	AVERAGE ANNUAL INTERNAL RATE OF RETURN (calculated)			0.98%	
31					

I have also entered sample contributions from February 28, 2001 to February 28, 2011 and the total market value of all RRSP accounts at December 31, 2012 – $100,000, in this example.

Have a look at the results in Figure 1.The first thing to notice is that the market value of your investments is greater than the amount invested by $5,400. Congratulations! You have a positive rate of return. In many cases, RRSP accounts are worth less than the actual dollars put into them. In this case the market value would be less than the contributions and there would be a negative rate of return.

But what rate of return have you received over the years in the example?

The PRR Calculator says ... 0.98 percent per year. Do your own calculation and put yourself in a much better position to decide whether to pay off your debts or continue with the RRSP strategy.

And if your broker says that it's too complicated for him or her to calculate the rate of return on your portfolio or that you wouldn't understand the complexities involved, bring your spreadsheet to the next meeting.

Summary

You're back to that all-important decision: investing versus paying down debt. Here are the steps you should take:

1. Use the PRR Calculator to calculate your RRSP average rate of return since inception.
2. Consider whether returns in the future will be as good.
3. List all your personal debts, including the interest rates.
4. Compare your expected RRSP returns to the rates on your debt. If the rates on your debt exceed what you think you'll earn in your RRSP, start attacking debt instead of handing any more money to your advisor.

Without the figure from Step 1, you're open to the smoke and mirrors so expertly used by many in the investment community to secure their own financial futures at your expense. Don't let that happen. Use the tools at your disposal to make the right decision for you and your family.

45

David Trahair

An Investment Primer

Before you put your money anywhere, be sure you understand the three basic principles of successful investing:

Asset allocation

Asset allocation is one of the keys to effective investing, and it's a simple concept. All it means is don't put all your eggs in one basket. If you do, you are assuming a huge amount of risk. Think back to January 2000. If you had sold everything you owned and put the proceeds solely in dot-com start-up companies, where would you be now? Put politely, that would have been an ineffective asset-allocation strategy.

Diversify by geography and investment type

With RRSPs, you should consider investing a portion outside Canada. Even if the Canadian market does well between now and your retirement, other countries may do even better.

With equities, you are assuming more risk because there is no guarantee that you will be able to sell your investment later for more than you bought it for. In the worst-case scenario, the company will go bankrupt, and you will get nothing. However, you might do well.

Make changes as you age

The older you are, the less risk you should be willing to take, because after your earnings stream is cut off, you can't afford a major decline in your investment value. You need to ensure you have sufficient funds to live.

5. Myth 4: We Have Met the Enemy, and He Is the Tax Collector

Exposing the Myth

Don't get me wrong. I'm not saying that you should enjoy paying your taxes. In fact, it's your right to reduce your taxes by legitimate means wherever possible. What I am saying is you shouldn't make financial decisions for tax reasons; you should make them for economic reasons, giving consideration to the tax effect of the situation.

Too often, a strong dislike of taxes leads unwary consumers into investing in misguided tax shelters, making poor choices about when to sell in the stock market, and making the ill-conceived decision to borrow to invest. Let's look at the reality.

Tax Shelters R Us

Tax shelters are number one on the list of products that prey on consumers' dislike for paying taxes. High-income earners, such as professional athletes, doctors, and lawyers, fall for this ploy time and time again. Investing in tax shelters is like playing the lottery. You may strike it rich, but odds are you'll lose – perhaps big time.

Here's the usual pitch: "Invest $10,000 in XYZ partnership and you'll get a $10,000 tax deduction! You could save more than $4,600 in taxes this year!"

That's great – if you get the $10,000 back later. The problem is that in the majority of cases, you won't. You may not get anything back. And if you don't, you have just thrown away $5,400 (in this example) or more, depending on your tax bracket. That's why the government is giving you the big tax break – because of the risk you are taking.

Why does the government allow these tax shelter schemes to exist? Mainly to encourage investment in certain industries. But you have to be aware also that the government does not support every tax shelter out there. They look very closely at tax shelters because many are simply shams. It is not uncommon for them to go back years and disallow deductions because a tax shelter turned out to be something less than legitimate.

If in the above example your deduction was disallowed, you would have lost the whole thing-not just $5,400, but $10,000 of your hard-earned cash. And if you had borrowed to make the investment, you would be making those loan payments for years to come and getting nothing in return.

Even worse, when the government reassesses your tax return, they will add interest to the additional taxes owing. In other words, you'll owe them the $4,600 in taxes, plus interest at the "prescribed interest rate" for every day since the taxes were originally due. (The prescribed interest rate is set quarterly by the government, and it is usually higher than the bank's prime rate.) Oh, and by the way, this interest isn't tax deductible.

It's not just traditional tax shelters that you have to watch out for. Let me give you an example.

Beware: Tax Shelter Ahead!

Near the end of December a couple of years ago, I started seeing ads in the paper for an "investment opportunity," but I had to hurry as there were only "four days left." On December 29, I decided to see what was being offered.

A well-known investment speaker was making a presentation about an "opportunity" to invest in a donation scheme. The reason for the big rush was because donations are deductible only if made by the end of the calendar year. During the presentation, videos and articles by esteemed professionals, including lawyers and accountants, were shown that claimed the government was on board with the scheme and that the group would fight any attempt to disallow the tax credits offered. They even had a $425,000 "defence fund" to fight the government if it changed its mind.

This is how it worked: If you invested $10,000, they would give you a donation receipt for $56,522 "based on fair market value." The money was being invested in comic books that would be used to help kids in developing countries learn to read. The group would buy the comic books in bulk and get a discount on the price, so that your $10,000 would actually buy $56,522 worth of comic books. Their calculations showed that you would receive a net tax credit of $15,427 – a return of over 50 percent on your original investment.

According to a September 2007 newspaper article, the Canada Revenue Agency (CRA) has targeted approximately 106,000 individual Canadians that have fallen for such donation schemes. The result can be ugly – in the article, one taxpayer and her husband admit they each donated $10,000 thinking they were helping children overseas. They got a significant tax break until CRA looked into their tax returns. The agency is now asking for over $70,000 to cover the disallowed donation, as well as interest, and penalties.

Here's the bottom line: If it sounds too good to be true, it is. Stay away from these scams no matter how tempted you are. They can lead to personal financial disaster.

Don't Sell: The Taxes Will Kill You

It is often said that investment decisions are based on two emotions: fear and greed. When the stock market is declining, fear drives people to sell to stop their losses. When the market is climbing, they hold onto their stocks hoping they'll go higher. Taxes can play a role in compounding the problem. A simple example from recent history will explain this.

Say you owned $1 million worth of Nortel stock at the peak of the market. That would have been 8,400 shares at about $120, equaling $1,008,000. At the time, you thought it might still go higher, so you waited. However, you called your accountant to see what the taxes would be just in case you did decide to sell. You had bought the stock at $25 per share, so your cost base was $210,000 (8,400 shares x $25). Your capital gain would have been the difference between the proceeds and the cost base: in this case, $798,000.

Capital gains get favourable tax treatment – only 50 percent of the actual gain is taxed – so in this case $399,000 would be added to your personal income tax return. Even if your salary was low, the amount would put the majority of the taxable capital gain in the top bracket. At a 46 percent marginal tax rate, you would have owed about $183,000 in taxes. "Get out!" you screamed at your accountant at the time, and you sat tight.

Today, the company is out of business your stock is worthless, but you no longer have a tax problem. Maybe you should have been less worried about tax!

David Trahair

Borrow Your Way to Riches – Or Rags

Some financial advisers promote the idea of borrowing to invest because the interest is tax deductible (for investments outside an RRSP). Once again, they are playing on your dislike of taxes, but they often don't reveal the risk associated with such a strategy.

Don't fall for this ploy. With a debt pay-down strategy, adding to your personal debt is a sin. If you have to borrow for a vacation, you are sacrificing your future for the present.

You may think that borrowing to invest isn't that bad, because you are using "leverage" to increase your net worth. Right? Well, you may find an investment that does well. Alternatively, you could end up broke.

Recent rates at a Canadian chartered bank tell the tale of how things are stacked against you. A five-year fixed term deposit pays 2.2 percent per year, while a five-year mortgage at the same institution costs 3.2 percent annually. That difference of 1 percent is called the "spread," and it's the way banks make much of their money. Since you're not the bank, you're working against the spread, and that's an uphill battle.

Can you imagine what the people who borrowed to invest in the stock market at the peak are wishing now? They will essentially have a mortgage on their future with no house attached. The concept is simple: Debt allows you to get into big trouble because you are risking more than you have. Unless you want to play the lottery with your family's future, don't do it.

The Alternative: Focus on Net Worth, Not Taxes

The problem with focusing on minimizing taxes is clear: It clouds your judgment and takes your attention away from other areas of your personal finances that could benefit you far more than saving a few tax dollars.

If you focus on building your net worth instead of just minimizing taxes, you'll likely make much wiser financial decisions. Spend more time thinking about the location in which you should buy your next house. Is it a good area? Do prices rise at a greater rate than one of your other options? When it comes time to sell, you'll have more cash in your pocket to put down on your next house.

If you own a business, focus on increasing its value. Your business has the potential to be a substantial portion of your total net worth and is a great way for you to provide funds for yourself after your retirement. You may be able to sell it or continue to take a salary or dividends after you stop working.

Once you start thinking this way, you'll probably come up with some of your own personal ideas – ideas that could make or save you a lot of money.

Summary

Focusing on your net worth is the key to making sound decisions, especially when it comes to taxes. If you do that, you will probably come to the same conclusions I have. Let's summarize:

- Investing in a tax shelter or donation scheme, no matter what your income level, is rarely a sound financial strategy.
- Don't borrow to invest inside or outside an RRSP.
- Never avoid the sale of an asset that has appreciated simply because you fear the tax bill.

6. Myth 5: Secure Your Financial Future: Buy Life Insurance

Exposing the Myth

For years, we've been exposed to ads from a certain insurance company about retiring early. The message is that if you put your trust in them, retirement at 55 is possible.

Now think about this: What has life insurance got to do with financial freedom? You won't achieve financial freedom. You'll be dead!

Life insurance does, however, have a vital purpose: It should allow a family to maintain their standard of living if the breadwinner were to die. If you talk to many life insurance agents however, you may get a different idea. The myths they perpetuate could cost you dearly.

The truth is that if you don't have any dependents, you really don't need any life insurance at all. If you have young children, you probably do need it. It boils down to what life would be like for your family without you.

Say you are a 35-year-old sole income-earner, with a spouse and two young children. If you were to die, what would they do? You probably wouldn't have a lot of money saved to sustain them for the rest of their lives. How would they pay for food, clothing, and shelter? You'd better have life insurance.

If, however, you have a working spouse but no children, why do you need life insurance? If you die, your spouse would probably continue working. Does it make sense for you to pay life insurance premiums so that if you die, your spouse's new companion could live off the death benefit and won't ever have to work?

The Case Against Whole Life and Universal Life Insurance

The box at the end of this chapter defines the three basic types of insurance available today: term, universal, and whole life. If you aren't familiar with these terms, take the time to review them now.

Many agents will try to sell you a universal life or a whole life insurance policy because of the "savings" component. They claim that you'll be building up savings at the same time as you cover your life. Don't fall for this argument. Let's look at the reasons why.

You Can't Have It Both Ways

With both whole and universal life insurance, you must remember this: You don't get the cash surrender value *and* the death benefit; you get the cash surrender value *or* the death benefit. The death benefit applies if the insured dies, and the cash surrender value applies if you cancel the policy.

In other words, the cash surrender value is being used to fund the death benefit. That's extremely important to keep in mind when you are looking at those fancy projections designed to sell you on these types of policies.

If You Cancel It, It's Not Tax-Free

If you cancel a whole or universal life insurance policy, you'll be taxed on the difference between the cash surrender value received and the cost base of the policy (you have to ask your insurance company for this value, but essentially it's the total premiums paid, less dividends received).

How Do Your Savings Grow?

Let's take a look at how effective the rate of return is on the savings invested in a life insurance policy. This is best explained by Kwok Ho and Chris Robinson in their excellent book, Personal Financial Planning (Captus Press, 2001):

Empirical studies in the past find that the rate of return on whole life is inferior to that available on comparable savings instruments. In other words, there is evidence that you would earn a higher return by putting the monetary "difference" in a chartered bank savings account than by putting it in whole life insurance. But why is that the case? We think this is due, to a large extent, to the high commission fees that insurance companies pay to agents. In general, the insurance companies pay a

David Trahair

much higher commission fee to agents for selling whole life than they do for selling individual term life. Since the commission is a percentage on the total premium that you pay, this means that you pay a commission for saving money with an insurance company. Banks do not charge you a commission for putting your money into a savings account![1]

How Big Is That Commission, Anyway?

If you have a whole life policy, you've probably paid thousands of dollars in premiums in a year, much more than you would have paid for term insurance. Just look at the cash surrender value at the end of the first year. It should be equal to, or more than, the excess you paid over the cost of simple term insurance. In many cases it's not, it's close to zero. That's because the insurance company's commission is often equal to almost all of the premiums you pay in that first year. Now you know why they are so aggressive in selling these types of policies.

When Will the Premiums Stop?

There are other significant risks with a universal or whole life policy. First of all, the premiums are not guaranteed. They could be extended for many years beyond what the charts show or even increased if the insurance company does not do as well as expected on its investments. Read the fine print and you'll see words like the following: "There is NO guarantee that regular premium payments and dump-ins can cease after eight years."

There is also no guarantee that the investment component will do better than the "guaranteed minimum" return. Insurance agents often state this by saying something like, "The primary example is based on the current dividend scale, which is not guaranteed."

Whole life policies are not at all flexible. The full premiums are due no matter what. At least with a universal life policy you can pay the pure cost of insurance out of dividends generated in the policy.

In short, it's difficult to make a strong independent recommendation for whole life insurance.

---

[1] Excerpted from *Personal Financial Planning*, 3rd ed., by Kwok Ho and Chris Robinson (Concord, Ontario: Captus Press Inc., 2001). Reprinted with permission of Captus Press Inc., Units 14 & 15, 1600 Steeles Ave. West, Concord, ON L4K 4M2. Email: Info@captus.com, Internet: www.captus.com.

How Much Coverage Do You Need?

Now that we've dispelled the myths of life insurance, let's look at how to determine the amount of coverage you should have.

Many people decide how much insurance to get because they are sold a policy by an aggressive salesperson. Here's one pitch I have heard:

- *Step 1:* Add up all your personal debt, including credit cards, lines of credit, mortgage, and car loans.
- *Step 2:* Determine the amount of money you would need to invest to replace the annual salary of the insured person.
- *Step 3:* Add the two amounts together, and that's the amount of coverage you need.

Let's throw some numbers in and see what happens using this method.

A couple, Bob and Sarah Simpson, have one child, Avril, age five, and personal debt, including a mortgage, totaling $250,000. Bob is the only breadwinner, and he makes $90,000 per year. Assuming an average rate of return of 5 percent, $1.8 million would be needed to generate $90,000 per year. Bob would need to insure himself for $2.05 million ($250,000 + $1.8 million), according to the pitch. If Bob qualifies, that's quite a hefty amount of coverage and would be very costly.

Are the Simpsons being well advised or is the sales person just doing a great selling job? Let's see.

First of all, they do need life insurance on Bob because if he were to die, Sarah and Avril would otherwise be in dire straights. But how much do they need?

There are two ways to determine the amount of coverage required: the income-replacement method and the expense-projection method. The former focuses on replacing the income that will be lost, and the latter focuses on the future expenses that need to be covered. Unfortunately, like most Canadian families, the Simpsons don't keep detailed records of their spending. They are therefore forced to focus on income replacement rather than the more accurate expense-projection method.

David Trahair

The Income-Replacement Method

With the income-replacement method, in our example, if Sarah were to receive $1.8 million on Bob's death, it would pay her $90,000 per year at 5 percent. As we saw in Chapter 2, this is a neat trick that is often used, but it's deceiving in its simplicity. Sarah would get the $90,000 every year and she would also be left with the $1.8 million intact when she died.

Assume Sarah is 35 years old when Bob dies. To provide $90,000 per year, assuming a 5 percent rate of return on the investments for the next 30 years, she would only need $1.4 million. That amount would yield $90,000 for 30 years. This is the time period that Bob would have been working had he lived.

But there is another important point to consider: taxes. The face value of a policy is received tax-free, since life insurance premiums are not tax deductible, and that makes a big difference. Bob would have been reporting the $90,000 per year as salary income and would have been paying income tax on the full amount if he had lived. Sarah would not have to include the $1.4 million death benefit in her income. She would, however, pay taxes on any interest earned on the face amount after it is paid out, but that would be much less than what Bob would have paid.

Look at it this way: Sarah would receive $2.7 million over the next 30 years ($90,000 x 30), but $1.4 million of that would simply be a return of her capital and therefore not taxed. Over the 30 years she would be paying tax on the difference ($1.3 million), whereas Bob would have paid tax on the whole $2.7 million. That means she would need a lot less coverage than the $1.4 million to be in the same position as Bob on an after-tax basis.

Many in the insurance industry use a factor of 75 percent to compensate for this tax issue. That is, they recommend you insure to replace only 75 percent of the lost income. In this case, 75 percent of $90,000 is $67,500. Sarah would still need $1.04 million of coverage to provide that much per year for 30 years at 5 percent. That's about half the amount the sales representative was pushing, but it is still a formidable amount.

The Expense-Projection Method

If the Simpsons diligently tracked their expenses, they could use the expense-projection method. With detailed information about past and current spending, it's not that difficult to project future spending. They would then probably notice several important things.

First of all, without Bob, their expenses would decline. There would be one less mouth to feed every day. They would need only one car. Sarah and Avril wouldn't require as much space and would have the option of downsizing the house. They would also need to save less for retirement. Avril will soon be six years old and starting grade one. That will leave Sarah more time, perhaps to get a job. She may even find another mate who already earns an income.

All these factors should be taken into consideration. The conclusion could very well be that a much lower amount of insurance is required.

Now assume that Sarah is already keen to get back to work. If they insured Bob for $250,000, the total amount of their debt, she would be able to clear it all if he died. As we saw in Chapter 2, if you have no debt, your expenses decline significantly. Even if Sarah doesn't earn as much as Bob does, she may be able to maintain her standard of living quite well upon his death.

Having said that, it makes sense to get several quotes for higher death benefits than you think you'll need. Often the increase in the premiums is not that significant and if that is the case you may wish to buy more insurance as a cushion.

Summary

Everyone's personal financial situation is different. There are no "right answers." If you don't have a good idea of where your money is going, and therefore how much insurance you need, you are leaving yourself vulnerable to the "rule of thumb" selling methods used by some less-than-objective agents. You can do better than that.

David Trahair

Understanding Insurance Basics

Beneficiary: The person to whom a death benefit is paid after the death of an insured person.

Face value: The amount received by the beneficiary upon the death of the insured. Also known as the death benefit.

Insurability: Whether or not a person qualifies for insurance. In most cases, a medical exam is required to determine whether or not an insurance company will assume the risk of insuring someone.

Owner: The person who pays the insurance premiums. This can be the insured, another person, or even a company.

Premium: The amount paid to the insurance company, usually on a monthly or annual basis.

Policy term: The period covered by the insurance policy. This can range from one year to a lifetime.

Rate: The cost of each unit of insurance. For example, a rate of $1.50 per $100 unit would translate to $375 annual cost for a $25,000 face value policy ($25,000/$100 x $1.50).

Types of Insurance Available

Term life: A pure life insurance policy without any savings/ investment features.

Universal life: A combination of term life insurance and a separate investment fund. As long as you pay the insurance portion of the premium each year, the policy remains in force. These policies are flexible because the amount accumulated in the investment fund can be used to pay the premium required to maintain the policy if you can't afford to do so.

Whole life: Similar to universal life, except the premiums are not segregated into an insurance premium and a savings component. You are leaving it up to the insurance company to handle all aspects of the policy, including the investments.

A term policy will have a much lower premium that increases with age. As you get older, the premiums become very expensive, to the point at which it does not make sense to continue coverage.

Policies with an investment component have premiums for a fixed period of time that eventually stop, even though the insurance coverage continues. You pay more than the required amount for the insurance coverage in the beginning, and less than the required amount toward the end of the policy. The excess funds in the early years are invested and accumulated by the insurance company. This is what's called the "cash surrender value" (CSV). If you cancel the policy, the cash surrender value is what will be returned to you. These types of policies are just a combination of term insurance and an investment account where the investment portion is used up in future years to pay for the coverage. They will pay the death benefit, assuming you continue to pay all the required premiums.

PART TWO: FIGHTING BACK

7. The RRSP Trap: Optimize, Don't Maximize

The RRSP Trap

Like many of us in the current economic climate, you've probably conceded that you aren't going to retire a multimillionaire. You just want to have a reasonable amount put away to ensure your golden years are comfortable. How much of an RRSP are you going to need? $300,000? $650,000? $1million? If you're like many Canadians, you simply have no idea. Unfortunately, the answer is not as easy as applying a rule of thumb, because we each have a financial situation that is as individual as our fingerprints.

How Much Money Will You Need?

Imagine for a minute that you are a track and field athlete entering the Olympic Games. Your specialty is running. You show up at the stadium for your race, but there's a problem: You have no idea how long the race is. Are you entered in the 100-yard dash or a marathon? It obviously makes a huge difference in terms of how you should have trained for the event. Training for a marathon isn't going to help much in a race that's over in 9.58 seconds.

That's how many people approach retirement. They know they are going to be in an event when they retire. In this case, the event is money management, and most people aren't very good at it. To take a page from one of my favourite books, *The 7 Habits of Highly Effective People* (Stephen R. Covey, Simon & Schuster), the best way to play this game is to begin with the end in mind. That is, determine about how much money you will spend each year, how long you are likely to live, and work backwards to determine how big your RRSP needs to be.

Without this personal information, what do most people do? They assume the maximum RRSP contribution levels are what they'll need to invest each year to secure their retirement. They live a stressed out existence feeling guilty that they don't seem to be able to maximize their RRSP contributions. But is maximizing the answer?

Let's dig deeper to find out.

RRSP Problem 1: Age 71

The federal budget of 2007 increased the mandatory age at which you must convert your RRSP to retirement income back up to 71 from 69. (71 was the age in effect prior to 1996.)

The current rules state that during the year you turn 71, you must convert your RRSP to a Registered Retirement Income Fund (RRIF) or annuity and begin withdrawing set amounts by December 31 of the next year. That next year, you will still be 71 at the beginning of the year and will turn 72 during the year. (Note that the RRIF rules are based on your age at the beginning of the year, not the age you turn during the year.) The minimum RRIF withdrawal percentage for the year you are 71 at the beginning is 7.38 percent of the opening market value of the RRIF. The next year, it's 7.48 percent.

Remember that if you have a younger spouse you can, if you can afford to, base your minimum withdrawal percentages on his or her age. If your spouse is under 71, you will need to base the withdrawal amount on the formula $1/(90 - \text{age})$ so $1/(90 - 69) = 0.0476$ for the year he/she started at age 69 and $1/(90-70) = 0.05$ for the year he/she started at age 70.

For the years when you are 71 to 77 at the beginning of the year, the formula no longer works for RRIFs opened after 1992. The rates have been set by the government and, as you probably guessed, they are higher than they otherwise would be. For example, for the year during which you are 71 at the beginning (and turn 72 during), the rate is 7.38 percent, not 5.26 percent, as the formula would dictate. Again, it's a way of getting more tax revenue out of your pockets sooner. The fixed percentage rises to 8.15 percent in the year you start at age 77 (the formula would dictate 7.69 percent in that year). For the year you start at age 78 and older, the rates are set by the government and gradually increase to 20 percent at age 94 and above.

One of the problems with these rules is that they penalize people who have their finances under control. What if you don't need that much money to live the way you would like? You don't have a choice; you must withdraw the minimum amount and pay tax on it.

Let's consider an example.

If you had a RRIF worth $1,000,000 at the beginning of the year you started at age 71, you would have to withdraw $73,800. What if you could get along comfortably on $50,000 because you have no debt, you own your cars and your kids are self-sufficient? You would have to pay tax on the extra $23,800 anyway, and that's about $7,600 at current 2012 Ontario rates.

The second problem is that a large RRIF may lead to clawbacks of the Old Age Security (OAS) pension.

In the above example, even without any other income (CPP, investments, etc.) the federal government would have clawed back $636 (15 percent of the excess above $69,562 in 2012). I don't know about you, but giving away free money doesn't sound like a good strategy to me.

RRSP Problem 2: Death

As long as you name your spouse or common-law partner as the successor annuitant in the terms of your RRIF contract or your will, your RRIF payments will continue to be paid to him or her after your death. Upon the demise of your spouse, however, the entire remaining balance of your RRIF comes into income on his or her final tax return, along with the balance of his or her own RRIF. (There is an exception for financially dependent children or grandchildren.) Often, the majority of this is at a high rate of tax.

For example, say the RRIFs had a fair market value of $400,000 immediately before the death of your surviving spouse. Even if he or she had no other income, the tax bill in Ontario would be about $166,000 in 2012.

Let's look at a scenario to see the effect of the OAS clawback and the taxation of RRIFs upon death.

Meet Jim Bradley

Jim Bradley was born on January 2, 1967, and is therefore 45 years old in 2012. Jim is good at what he does to earn income, but by his own admission, he lacks financial expertise. Securing his retirement years is simple in his mind, since it's what he's been hearing since he was a kid: Maximize RRSP contributions each and every year, no matter what. He has been doing just that since he was 30 years old.

(Okay, so if he had been really listening, he would have started at age 22; but he resisted and enjoyed the next eight years free of worry about retirement.)

In 1997, when he turned 30, he contributed the maximum allowed to the RRSP – $13,500. He continued doing that every year until 2012, where he contributed the maximum – $22,970. At an average annual rate of return of 5 percent, his RRSP portfolio was worth $385,975 at December 31, 2012.

Assuming he puts in the maximum allowed $23,820 from 2013 until 2032 (when he turns 65), and that the portfolio grows at 5 percent a year on average, his RRSP will grow to a value of $1,811,738 at December 31, 2032.

He plans to retire when he is 65 and begin collecting the CPP and OAS pensions at that time.

Jim wishes to know the following:

- Will his minimum RRIF payments exceed what he'll need to live comfortably?
- How much OAS pension will be clawed back after he retires?
- What will his RRIF be worth upon his death?
- How much tax will be payable on the RRIF on his final tax return?

To answer Jim's questions, we need to make some assumptions. Let's do that now.

The Assumptions

- Jim is eligible for the maximum OAS pension, which at present in 2012 is $6,540, and the amount will grow at the assumed inflation rate.
- Jim is eligible for the maximum CPP pension, which at present in 2012 is $11,840, and the amount will grow at the assumed inflation rate.
- Jim will require approximately 50 percent of his last year's pre-retirement income to maintain his lifestyle after he retires because his mortgage will be paid off, his kids will have moved out, and he will no longer be saving for retirement. In today's dollars, that is $50,000 (2012 income of $100,000 x 50 percent). This amount is adjusted for inflation.
- Jim will not have any other income after retirement (i.e., from company pensions, self-employment income, or investments outside his RRSP).

- The taxable income at which the OAS clawback begins is $69,562 in 2012, and this amount will increase at the assumed rate of inflation.
- Jim's RRSP/RRIF will earn an average of 4 percent per year after he retires, since he is shifting to more conservative investments.
- Inflation will average 2 percent per year from now until Jim dies.
- Jim will live until he is 85.
- His wife is the same age as Jim, and she does not out-live him.
- Federal and Ontario personal income taxes are calculated at 2011 rates.

The Results

Now let's look at Jim's spreadsheet, which is shown on the following pages as Figure 2.

The clawback of the OAS pension seems to be a problem for Jim from age 72 starting at $8,741 and declining until age 81. In total he will have to pay back $54,670.

The real problems arise when we look at some of the other columns. Have a look at the amount of RRIF income Jim will have to withdraw above what he has determined he'll need in the year he turns 72. The Total Income after Additional RRIF is $177,007. This amount includes the minimum RRIF payment, OAS and CPP pensions (there is no additional RRIF income required in this case). Now look at the Required Income – it's only $85,344. (For the technically inclined, that's 50 percent of the future value of his current salary of $100,000 for 27 years at 2 percent inflation per year). The difference is $91,663. That's extra income that Jim will have to withdraw and pay tax on, even though he doesn't need the money. Look at the Excess Income column on the far right. It shows the real problem with RRSPs that are too large. In Jim's case, from age 72 to 85, he will be forced to withdraw and pay tax on $888,843 of money he doesn't even need.

What about when Jim dies? If he dies at age 85, his RRIF will still be worth $1,001,435, and that'll cost him about $465,000 in taxes in Ontario in 2012.

What if he dies at 80? His RRIF will be worth an astounding $1,341,339. The tax bill on that? About $629,000.

Figure 2: RETIREMENT OPTIMIZER

RRSP YEARS

Age During Year**	RRSP Value Beginning of Year	RRSP Withdrawals	Increase in RRSP Value During Year	RRSP Value End of Year	OAS Payments*	CPP Payments*
55	0	0	0	0		
56	0	0	0	0		
57	0	0	0	0		
58	0	0	0	0		
59	0	0	0	0		
60	0	0	0	0		0
61	0	0	0	0		0
62	0	0	0	0		0
63	0	0	0	0		0
64	0	0	0	0		0
65	1,811,738	47,073	70,587	1,835,251	9,630	17,594
66	1,835,251	48,015	71,489	1,858,726	9,823	17,945
67	1,858,726	48,975	72,390	1,882,140	10,019	18,304
68	1,882,140	49,955	73,287	1,905,473	10,220	18,670
69	1,905,473	50,954	74,181	1,928,700	10,424	19,044
70	1,928,700	51,973	75,069	1,951,797	10,633	19,425
71	1,951,797	53,012	75,951	1,974,736	10,845	19,813

RRIF YEARS

Age During Year***	RRIF Value Beginning of Year	Minimum RRIF Withdrawals	Additional RRIF Withdrawal to Meet Required Income	Increase in RRIF Value During Year	RRIF Value End of Year	OAS Payments*
72	1,974,736	145,736	0	73,160	1,902,160	11,062
73	1,902,160	142,282	0	70,395	1,830,274	11,284
74	1,830,274	138,918	0	67,654	1,759,010	11,509
75	1,759,010	135,620	0	64,936	1,688,326	11,739
76	1,688,326	132,534	0	62,232	1,618,024	11,974
77	1,618,024	129,280	0	59,550	1,548,294	12,214
78	1,548,294	126,186	0	56,884	1,478,992	12,458
79	1,478,992	123,200	0	54,232	1,410,024	12,707
80	1,410,024	120,275	0	51,590	1,341,339	12,961
81	1,341,339	117,367	0	48,959	1,272,931	13,221
82	1,272,931	114,436	0	46,340	1,204,834	13,485
83	1,204,834	111,688	0	43,726	1,136,872	13,755
84	1,136,872	108,912	0	41,118	1,069,078	14,030
85	1,069,078	106,159	0	38,517	1,001,435	14,310
86	0	0	0	0	0	0
87	0	0	0	0	0	0
88	0	0	0	0	0	0
89	0	0	0	0	0	0
90	0	0	0	0	0	0
91	0	0	0	0	0	0
92	0	0	0	0	0	0
93	0	0	0	0	0	0
94	0	0	0	0	0	0
95	0	0	0	0	0	0

* Amounts adjusted for inflation
** You must convert your RRSP to a RRIF in the year you turn 71.
The next year you must make your first RRIF withdrawal before December 31st. During this next year you are 71 at the beginning of the year and you turn 72 during the year.

Other Income*	Total Income	OAS Clawback*	Total Income	Required Income*	RRSP on Death
0	0	0	0	0	0
0	0	0	0	0	0
0	0	0	0	0	0
0	0	0	0	0	0
0	0	0	0	0	0
0	0	0	0	0	0
0	0	0	0	0	0
0	0	0	0	0	0
0	0	0	0	0	0
0	0	0	0	0	0
0	74,297	0	74,297	74,297	0
0	75,783	0	75,783	75,783	0
0	77,299	0	77,299	77,299	0
0	78,845	0	78,845	78,845	0
0	80,422	0	80,422	80,422	0
0	82,030	0	82,030	82,030	0
0	83,671	0	83,671	83,671	0

CPP Payments*	Other Income*	Total Income Before Add. RRIF	Total Income After Add. RRIF	OAS Clawback*	Total Income	Required Income*	Excess Income	RRIF on Death	Regular Income Death Year	Total Income Death Year
20,210	0	177,007	177,007	8,741	168,266	85,344	91,663	0	0	0
20,614	0	174,179	174,179	7,960	166,218	87,051	87,128	0	0	0
21,026	0	171,453	171,453	7,188	164,265	88,792	82,661	0	0	0
21,447	0	168,806	168,806	6,421	162,385	90,568	78,238	0	0	0
21,875	0	166,383	166,383	5,679	160,704	92,379	74,004	0	0	0
22,313	0	163,807	163,807	4,907	158,900	94,227	69,580	0	0	0
22,759	0	161,403	161,403	4,153	157,250	96,112	65,292	0	0	0
23,214	0	159,122	159,122	3,410	155,712	98,034	61,088	0	0	0
23,679	0	156,915	156,915	2,670	154,245	99,994	56,921	0	0	0
24,152	0	154,740	154,740	1,926	152,814	101,994	52,746	0	0	0
24,635	0	152,557	152,557	1,173	151,384	104,034	48,522	0	0	0
25,128	0	150,571	150,571	441	150,130	106,115	44,456	0	0	0
25,631	0	148,573	148,573	0	148,573	108,237	40,335	0	0	0
26,143	0	146,613	146,613	0	146,613	110,402	36,211	1,001,435	146,613	1,148,048
0	0	0	0	0	0	0	0	0	0	0
0	0	0	0	0	0	0	0	0	0	0
0	0	0	0	0	0	0	0	0	0	0
0	0	0	0	0	0	0	0	0	0	0
0	0	0	0	0	0	0	0	0	0	0
0	0	0	0	0	0	0	0	0	0	0
0	0	0	0	0	0	0	0	0	0	0
0	0	0	0	0	0	0	0	0	0	0
0	0	0	0	0	0	0	0	0	0	0
				54,670		**TOTALS**	888,843	1,001,435	146,613	1,148,048

69

Your personal situation will almost certainly be different than Jim's, but there is a useful lesson that can be learned: perhaps you should concentrate on optimizing the amount of your RRSP rather than trying to maximize it.

How to Avoid the RRSP Trap

Let's take a look at what Jim Bradley could do to avoid the RRSP trap. Let's start by looking at the positive things that Jim has going for him with his current strategy of maximizing his RRSP contributions. First of all, he is getting a tax refund on his RRSP contribution. In 2012, he contributed the maximum $22,970, resulting in a tax refund of approximately $9,900 (a marginal tax rate of about 43 percent in Ontario).

Since he has already maximized his RRSP contributions, he can't reinvest the refund in his RRSP as we assumed the Harts did earlier. Good news for Jim – he gets to spend it on whatever he likes. For Jim, that's a European vacation each and every year. Obviously, there is some value in this situation. He is saving more than enough for retirement and getting a great vacation to boot, right? Well, yes. But is there perhaps a better way to do it?

We've seen the negatives of the situation – an RRSP that's so big at the end that Jim ends up having to withdraw more than he needs from his RRIF starting at age 72, clawbacks of the OAS pension, and resulting huge tax bill when he (or his spouse if she lives longer) dies. As we have also discussed, he is hoping for a 5 percent return on his RRSP investments, and may get that, but there are no guarantees.

Let's look at what Jim could do differently. If he reduces his RRSP contributions to $8,000 per year, his RRSP refund at 43 percent would be about $3,400. So instead of handing over $22,970 to his mutual fund salesperson and getting $9,900 back from the government (a net cash outflow of $13,070), he hands $8,000 over and gets $3,440 back, for a net outflow of $4,560.

Assuming he started with $22,970 available, the reduced RRSP option would leave him with $18,410. That's the extra $14,970 that he didn't hand over, plus the $3,440 tax refund. He has $8,510 more in hand than with the maximum RRSP option. He can do whatever he likes with it. He could invest it in something other than an RRSP or choose to purchase something like a vacation property.

I can hear the mutual fund salespeople screaming already. With the maximum RRSP strategy he's got an extra $14,970 working in his RRSP for him! What about the value of compound earnings? And what about the fact that the money is growing tax sheltered?

The result of all those "positives" is that he ends up with a huge RRSP that penalizes him because he has his finances under control and doesn't need all that money after retirement. Furthermore, he doesn't feel inclined to hand over almost half of what's left in his RRIF after he dies to the taxperson.

But let's not stop there. We need to know if Jim has enough to retire on with the reduced RRSP contributions. I have punched in Jim's new answers to the spreadsheet, and guess what? He's fine. His RRSP will still grow to $1,2886634 by age 65, he will always meet his required income levels, and when he dies at age 85 his RRIF will still be worth $651,521.

The Retirement Optimizer Key Variables

There are some variables relating to retirement over which you have little control: inflation, the age you will pass to the great beyond, and income tax rates, to name a few.

There are others, however, over which you have a great deal of control, such as the percentage of your current income that you will need after you retire.

As we have seen, if you retire debt-free with self-sufficient children and are in reasonably good physical shape, that percentage could be 50 percent or even lower. On the other hand, if you retire in debt up to your ears, keep wasting money on trivial things, and have live-at-home kids, you could need even more than you make now! The choice is not easy, but it's yours to make.

There is also another variable that you control. It's whether you can, or will need to, earn income after you retire. Unfortunately for some, it will be a requirement. They simply won't have enough money put aside to survive. For others, it's worth giving some thought to.

What Are You Doing after Work?

No, I don't mean at 5:00 p.m. (or 7:00p.m. or 8:00p.m. if you are a workaholic); I mean after you stop working for good. I mean what are your hobbies? You'll need to do something to keep yourself busy, and that something you definitely have control over. It can also have a huge impact on how much money you'll need.

Think about your hobby: is it a cash generator, a cash drainer, or cash neutral? Many hobbies are cash drainers, including such things as travelling the world, becoming a wine connoisseur, or perhaps collecting fine art. There is absolutely nothing wrong with those hobbies; they'll just cost you more. Cash neutral (more or less) hobbies could include gardening, photography, woodworking, automobile restoration, volunteering on nonprofit boards, etc.

Cash-generating hobbies could include consulting in your area of expertise, lecturing, or perhaps writing or handyman activities. Sitting around the house all day would drive me nuts. I love dealing with money issues and hope to continue writing and giving courses on the subject even after I stop working full time. That will be a source of funds for me. What about you?

Let's go back to Jim Bradley and plug in some numbers to see what happens. We'll assume that Jim feels he'll be able to earn $5,000 per year (in today's dollars) from age 66 to 70. That will reduce the amount he will need to withdraw from his RRSP during those years before he has to convert his RRSP to an RRIF. Let's say that because of this, he figures he can afford to reduce his RRSP contributions from $8,000 to $5,000 per year. The results?

His RRSP will be worth $1,189,436 at age 65, he will always meet his required income estimate, and his RRIF will still be worth $607,616 at age 85.

How to Optimize Your Own RRSP

Jim Bradley's case showed us that if we get our finances under control, we might not need to maximize our RRSP contributions. In Chapter 2, we looked at the Harts and showed how in some cases, it may be possible to finance our retirement years with a very small RRSP. Your case probably won't be like Jim Bradley or the Harts since you and your family are unique and your situation will change, in some cases almost daily.

To help you, the spreadsheet we have been using for Jim Bradley is available to you free of charge. It's called the "Retirement Optimizer" and it is not password protected. All you have to do is just go to my website at www.trahair.com and click on "Smoke and Mirrors" on the left hand side. (You will need to have Microsoft Excel installed on your computer or you can go to www.openoffice.org to download a free spreadsheet program that will run all the spreadsheets).

After you open the file, simply answer the same questions that Jim Bradley did earlier in this chapter. The spreadsheet will do the rest.

Here's a list of the questions you'll need to answer:

- What is today's date?
- What is your first and last name?
- On what day were you born?
- In what province or territory do you reside?
- What is the total market value of your RRSPs on the most recent statement?
- How much do you plan to contribute to your RRSP each year from now until retirement?
- At what age do you plan to retire and stop making RRSP contributions?
- At what annual rate of return do you expect your RRSP investments to grow until you retire?
- At what annual rate of return do you expect your RRSP or RRIF investments to grow after you retire?
- What average annual rate of inflation do you expect over the remainder of your life?
- Are you eligible for the maximum Old Age Security (OAS) pension at age 65? If not, how many years will you have lived in Canada since age 18 when you are 65?
- Are you eligible for the maximum Canada Pension Plan (CPP) pension at age 65? If not, what has your average annual income from earnings been since you turned 18? Would you like to start receiving your CPP pension between the ages of 60 and 65? If so, at what age would you like to start?
- How much money from other sources in today's dollars do you expect each year after you retire? (For example, pension, self-employment, rental, and investments outside RRSPs.)
- At what age do you expect this income from other sources to stop?
- What is your current total income before taxes? (i.e., salary or net income from self-employment)

- What percentage of your income before tax in today's dollars do you think you will need after you retire?
- To what age do you think you will live? (Note: If you have a spouse who you think will live longer than you, enter the age you would have been at the time of his or her death.)

The program will then calculate all your numbers each year from age 55 to 95 including:

- What your RRSP will be worth when you retire and every year thereafter;
- Your required income, adjusted for inflation;
- CPP and OAS income, also adjusted for inflation;
- The amount of any OAS clawback;
- The minimum RRIF withdrawal amounts you will be required to make;
- The year-by-year RRSP and RRIF values, taking into account investment returns and withdrawals;
- How much your RRSP or RRIF will still be worth when you die; and
- The approximate personal income taxes that would be payable on the RRSP/RRIF value on your death.

Remember when you do your own retirement optimizer to do one for yourself and a separate one for your spouse as it is designed to track the income of retirement for individuals, not couples.

Even if you are not that comfortable with computers, Microsoft Excel, or personal finance, I encourage you to give it a try – it's easy to use! If you are comfortable with it, keep it up to date by changing the figures you input as your situation changes (for example, investment rates of return, inflation, percentage of income you will require after you retire).

Don't Forget Pension Income Splitting

While the retirement optimizer is not designed to factor in the tax implications of retirement, at this point it is important to note a fairly recent change in tax policy that could have a significant impact on the amount of tax you pay in retirement – the ability to split pension income.

Beginning with 2007 income tax returns, Canadian residents will generally be able to allocate up to 50 percent of their income that qualifies for the existing pension income tax credit to their resident spouse or common-law partner for tax purposes.

The amount allocated is deducted in determining the net income of the person who actually received the pension income, and added to the net income of the spouse or common-law partner.

Old Age Security and Canada Pension Plan payments do not qualify but the following do:

- The taxable part of annuity payments from a super-annuation or pension fund or plan; and
- If received as a result of the death of a spouse or common-law partner, or if the pensioner is age 65 or older at the end of the year:
  - Annuity and registered retirement income fund (including life income fund) payments; and
  - Registered retirement savings plan annuity payments.

Make sure your tax preparer is familiar with this new tax break – a simple allocation of pension income from a high income to a low-income spouse could save thousands of dollars in in tax.

8. Making the Right Choices by Using the Right Tools

Now that you understand the myths that may be used to fool you out of your hard-earned money, you need to know what to do about it. How can you turn the tables, take control, and fight back?

Knowledge Is a Tool

In the world of personal financial planning, as in most other parts of life, knowledge is key. It's difficult to dispute the messages you hear every day about what to do with your money if you don't understand what is being said.

If you haven't been trained in money matters for either your job or your own interest, you need to resolve now to devote some time to financial learning. Check out your library or local bookstore, subscribe to a financial magazine, and follow the financial writers in your favourite daily newspaper.

Just get interested. If you don't, you are a sitting duck against the slick messages launched at you by the multi-million-dollar advertising arms of the big financial institutions.

Your Best Friend: A Business Calculator

In addition to knowledge, there is one tool you will find indispensable in your quest for financial freedom: a good business calculator. It will allow you to experiment with different scenarios in saving for retirement as well as to calculate all the variables in any type of loan arrangement.

You can purchase a business calculator at any well-stocked business or stationery store. Look for one that has a large, ten-digit readout and which comes with an instruction manual. This inexpensive item (you can expect to pay about $30 to $50) will be worth its weight in gold. It will allow you to calculate future value of money, compounding interest rates, and much more. You'll also find that they are easy to learn how to use. Just follow the instructions that come with the model you choose. (Also see the boxes at the end of this chapter for more information on the basics of using a business calculator.)

Calculating the Future: Example

Here's a simple example that will show you how having a business calculator in your back pocket can help you fight back with both knowledge and tools:

Allyson and Sue are both 22 years old. They have both heard the sales pitch: "Start saving now for retirement or else!"

Allyson buys into the pitch and invests $2,000 a year for six years, and then she stops when she quits her job to stay home for a few years with her small child.

Sue, on the other hand, chooses to spend some of her money on herself for a few years. She travels around the world and works in a variety of jobs before settling down. She starts investing seven years later, and she, too invests $2,000 a year, but she manages to do so for the next 37 years.

Both women earn 12 percent on their investments. When Allyson and Sue reach age 65, who will be further ahead? The one who started early and interrupted her savings plan, or the one who waited a few years? With a business calculator, you can find the answer easily.

- For Allyson, you first need to calculate the future value of the annuity of $2,000 per year for six years. Answer: $16,230.38. Then you need to calculate the future value of that single amount for 37 years. Answer: $1,074,967.98.
- For Sue, you need to calculate the future value of an annuity of $2,000 for 37 years. Answer: $1,087,197.38.

As you can see, both women end up with about $1 million, but Sue comes out a little bit ahead over 43 years (by $12,229.40).

Without a business calculator, it's very difficult to make these calculations and even harder to argue with a salesperson who is trying to convince you that one strategy is better than another. But with a business calculator in hand, you've got the power to check the figures and, more importantly, to plug in your own figures. After all, it's your figures that count, not a canned example.

For instance, forget about a 12 percent annual return. Those days are history. What happens if it's only 5 percent? The future value in both cases is only about $203,000 – a lot less appealing.

David Trahair

The Low Monthly Lease Trap

With a business calculator, you can protect yourself against a devious method of consistently draining your bank account: the low monthly lease trap.

Whether it's cars, couches, appliances, or computers, consumers are constantly bombarded by ads for high-priced items promoting low monthly lease payments. It's all so painless isn't it? In some cases they don't even tell you the cost of the item. Without knowing the cost, it's virtually impossible to determine whether you're getting a good deal or not. Leasing is one of the ways companies can play games and record a handsome profit without your even knowing you've been taken.

You may have heard an old rule of thumb that you should buy things that appreciate and lease things that depreciate. If this were the case, you would always lease everything from a car to a computer because they decline in value over time.

Unfortunately, it's not that simple. The answer totally depends on the specifics of the situation. Let's look at the example of a computer.

If you lease a computer, you'll have to give it back at the end of the lease or buy it out. If you purchase it, it's yours to keep. Before you even consider the numbers, think about the difference in those two options. After two or three years your computer will be very outdated.

If you run a business that requires current technology, you'll need a new one. Who is going to use the old one? The kids? Forget it; they probably need more power than you to run all their games and peripherals. When you get a new one, you probably won't even touch the old one again. Face it: your old computer is a boat anchor. If it's going to be that useless, why buy it? Leasing seems like the obvious answer, but is it?

Let's look at a real-life example of what it may cost to lease. Here are the facts:

- Estimated cost: $3,458.00
- Lease term: 36 months
- Monthly lease payment: $127.78
- Estimated purchase option price at end of lease term: fair market value

The last point is the wild card. What is the fair market value going to be after three years? They don't say in the contract, but in a previous lease it was 15 percent of the cost, so we'll assume it's $518.70 ($3,458 x 15 percent).

The important point to note with leases is that since you don't own the item in the end, you are not financing the whole cost of the item. You have to discount the end-of-lease buyout amount (at the incremental cost of borrowing). The present value of $518.70 at a discount rate of, say, 5 percent, is $448.07.

In this case, you are financing only $3,009.93 ($3,458.00 – $448.07). On your business calculator, you can compute the internal rate of return that this lease is costing:

- The present value is $3,009.93.
- The number of payments is 36.
- The payment amount is $127.78.
- The monthly interest cost is 2.5 percent. The annual interest rate is a whopping 30 percent (2.5 x 12).

The interest amount over the 36-month term is the difference between the total payments of $4,600.08 (36 x $127.78) and the amount being financed ($3,009.93).

In all, that's $1,590.15 in interest over three years for the use of the computer, and you don't even own it at the end!

Look at it another way. If you took out a loan to purchase this computer at a rate of 7 percent a year, your monthly payments would be only $106.77, and you would then own it.

The moral of the story is to beware. Leasing can be very deceiving, and a business calculator won't let you down!

The Basics of Using a Business Calculator

Finance is based on the concept of the time value of money. A dollar in your hands today is worth more than a dollar you'll get a year from now. The underlying basis for any calculation concerning the time value of money is rate of return.

Here are the terms and abbreviations with which you should become familiar to use your business calculator:

- PV: present value of money
- FV: future value of money
- i: interest rate per compounding period
- n: number of compounding periods
- PMT: the payment amount (for a series of payments)

Let's look at how these terms are used in an example:

Example: The Power of Compounding

If you have $100 today and you put the money into a term deposit earning 5 percent per year, you will have $105 at the end of the year. That's $100 in principal, plus $5 in interest. In this case, the present value (PV) is $100, the interest rate (i) is 5 percent per year (or per annum), the compounding period (n) is 1, and the future value (FV) is $105. Put another way, the present value of a future value of $105 discounted at a rate of 5 percent for one year is $100.

In most cases, you will be dealing with more than one period in your calculations, and that's where the concept of compounding comes in. Compounding refers to how often the interest amount comes into the calculation. Say you invested the $100 for 5 years at 5 percent per year. At the end of the first year, you would have $105; but at the end of the second year, you would have $110.25 since the $105 at the end of the first year would be earning 5 percent for the second year. That's $5.25; $5.00 on the principal of $100 and $0.25 on the $5 of interest.

The third year, you'd have $115.76; the fourth, $121.55; and at the end of five years, you would have $127.63.

9. Your Mortgage: Friend or Foe?

If you're like most people, you probably think that you should try to reduce your expenses so you can spend more on the things you want and save for a decent retirement. There are many who argue that the way to do this is to reduce your daily expenses. Skip that cup of Tim Hortons coffee on the way to work. Forget that trip to the zoo and let the kids play in the backyard instead. Pack a lunch rather than buying one.

Is this really an effective strategy? Surely there's a better way than eliminating all the small indulgences that make life a little brighter. Instead, why not give some thought to the biggest expenses you'll ever have and reduce them instead?

Your mortgage is probably going to be the most significant debt you will ever incur. The decisions you make regarding your mortgage will, therefore, have a huge impact on your financial situation. The problem is that the various options are confusing, and as a result people often just accept whatever their bank offers. Don't do this. You could be throwing away thousands, perhaps even tens of thousands, of your hard-earned dollars.

Mortgage Basics

To understand the essential elements of a mortgage, let's start with a simple example and work through the different components.

Say you bought a house for $200,000 using $50,000 of your own money and borrowing the remaining $150,000. That means the opening principal balance of the mortgage would be $150,000.

Assume the mortgage was at a 5 percent annual interest rate for a five-year term and was being amortized over 25 years. The bank tells you that your monthly payments are $872.41. Is that right? You won't know unless you have an amortization schedule.

Using an Amortization Schedule

An amortization schedule is a detailed spreadsheet that shows the interest and principal portion of each payment for the entire life of a mortgage.

David Trahair

You will need to know the following to produce an accurate amortization schedule:

- Interest rate
- Term
- Amortization period
- Compounding method (daily, monthly, semi-annually, annually, etc.)

You can produce an amortization schedule by using a basic software program that will print out a full amortization schedule for any period-even a 30-year mortgage. It shows all details to the penny and is flexible enough to include special payments at any time. If you have an amortization software program, you will be able to compare alternatives before choosing a mortgage, and that can potentially save you a lot of money.

Don't use the amortization "quick and dirty" calculators found on a myriad of financial websites. It's worth investing in a proper program that allows you to plug in different interest rates, amortization periods, and monthly payments to see which option suits you best. (The program I have been using for years is an excellent one called MORTGAGE2 PRO. It was written by a Canadian engineer, Ron Cirotto, and is available through his website at www.amortization.com.)

Key Mortgage Variables

There are several key variables in a mortgage to consider. Figure 3, a screen shot from the first page of the amortization schedule for our example, illustrates these.

You can see under the "Payment" column that the first monthly blended payment is $872.41, which consists of $618.59 in interest and $253.82 in principal. The "Balance" column shows that there is $149,746.18 remaining on the mortgage after that first payment (the original balance of $150,000 less the $253.82 principal portion of the first payment).

Figure 3
MORTGAGE AMORTIZATION SCHEDULE

Date	Days	Pmt #	Payment	Int %	Interest	Principal	Balance	Prepay	Acc. Int	Notes
2/1/2012	31	1	872.41	5.0000	618.59	253.82	149,746.18	.00	618.59	
3/1/2012	29	2	872.41	5.0000	617.54	254.87	149,491.31	.00	1,236.13	
4/1/2012	32	3	872.41	5.0000	616.49	255.92	149,235.39	.00	1,852.62	
5/1/2012	30	4	872.41	5.0000	618.43	256.98	148,978.41	.00	2,468.05	
6/1/2012	31	5	872.41	5.0000	614.37	258.04	148,720.37	.00	3,082.42	
7/1/2012	30	6	872.41	5.0000	613.31	259.10	148,461.27	.00	3,695.73	
8/1/2012	31	7	872.41	5.0000	612.24	260.17	148,201.10	.00	4,307.97	
9/1/2012	31	8	872.41	5.0000	611.17	261.24	147,939.86	.00	4,919.14	
10/1/2012	30	9	872.41	5.0000	610.09	262.32	147,677.54	.00	5,529.23	
11/1/2012	31	10	872.41	5.0000	609.01	263.40	147,414.14	.00	6,138.24	
12/1/2012	30	11	872.41	5.0000	607.92	264.49	147,149.66	.00	6,746.16	
1/1/2013	32	12	872.41	5.0000	606.83	265.58	146,884.07	.00	7,352.99	
2/1/2013	31	13	872.41	5.0000	605.74	266.67	146,617.40	.00	7,958.73	
3/1/2013	28	14	872.41	5.0000	604.64	267.77	146,349.63	.00	8,563.37	
4/1/2013	31	15	872.41	5.0000	603.63	268.88	146,080.75	.00	9,166.98	
5/1/2013	30	16	872.41	5.0000	602.42	269.99	145,810.76	.00	9,769.32	
6/1/2013	31	17	872.41	5.0000	601.31	271.10	145,539.66	.00	10,370.63	
7/1/2013	30	18	872.41	5.0000	600.19	271.22	145,267.44	.00	10,970.82	
8/1/2013	31	19	872.41	5.0000	599.07	273.34	144,994.10	.00	11,569.89	
9/1/2013	31	20	872.41	5.0000	597.94	274.47	144,719.63	.00	12,167.83	
10/1/2013	30	21	872.41	5.0000	596.81	275.60	144,444.03	.00	12,764.64	
11/1/2013	31	22	872.41	5.0000	595.67	276.74	144,167.29	.00	13,360.31	
12/1/2013	30	23	872.41	5.0000	594.63	277.88	143,889.41	.00	13,954.84	
1/1/2014	31	24	872.41	5.0000	593.39	279.02	143,610.39	.00	14,548.23	
2/1/2014	31	25	872.41	5.0000	592.24	280.17	143,330.22	.00	15,140.47	
3/1/2014	28	26	872.41	5.0000	591.08	281.33	143,048.89	.00	15,731.56	
4/1/2014	31	27	872.41	5.0000	589.92	282.49	142,766.40	.00	16,321.47	
5/1/2014	30	28	872.41	5.0000	588.76	283.65	142,482.75	.00	16,910.23	
6/1/2014	31	29	872.41	5.0000	587.59	284.82	142,197.93	.00	17,497.82	
7/1/2014	30	30	872.41	5.0000	586.41	286.00	141,911.93	.00	18,084.23	
2012 total	91	3	2,101.26		1,722.84	378.42		.00		

Last Payment on 1/1/2037

Figure 3, MORTGAGE2 PRO, copyright © 2012 is used by permission of Ron Cirotto.

Total Interest

Now look at the line just above all the columns in Figure 3. There you will see the total interest that you would pay on this mortgage for the entire amortization period. It's $111,721.44. That figure is key in mortgage comparisons because it summarizes the big picture – exactly what the mortgage will cost you over its life.

David Trahair

Effective Interest Rate

Amortization programs can also show the effective interest rate (EIR). In Figure 3, you can see it to the right of the annual interest rate: an EIR of 5.0625. But why is it higher than 5 percent, the annual interest rate of the mortgage? The answer has to do with compounding frequency.

Canadian residential mortgages are stated at an annual interest rate with semi-annual compounding. By law, they can't be compounded more frequently than that. The compounding period is six months, while the repayment period is usually monthly or biweekly, which results in an effective annual interest rate being higher than the annual interest rate.

Let's look at the 5 percent annual rate used in the example. For the first six months, you pay 5 percent x 6/12, which is 2.5 percent, so the factor is 1.025 percent for that period. For the next six months, you would pay 2.5 percent on the 1.025 percent, and that's 1.025 x 1.025, which equals 1.050625. The annual effective interest rate is therefore 1.050625 minus 1, which equals 5.0625 percent.

Remember that the compounding frequency is the number of times during a period, usually a year, that the interest component comes into the transaction. With investments, you are better off with more frequent compounding, because the interest you have earned in the first compounding period (but haven't received yet) is added to the investment principal balance, and the interest for the next period is calculated on the combination of the two.

With mortgages the opposite is true. The lender is the investor and you are the borrower. Sorry, you lose.

Days per Year

Another key factor in mortgage calculations is the days per year. Everyone knows there are 365 days in a year and 366 in a leap year; but with a mortgage, you can select either 360 or 365 (see the box in the upper right-hand corner in Figure 3). The reason for selecting 360 days is that in banking circles, the year is often divided into 12 equal 30-day months. The total is 360.

In Canada prior to 1984, almost all mortgages were monthly payment mortgages using a 360-day year. After 1984, weekly and biweekly payment mortgages were introduced and along with that came another method of calculating mortgages: the exact day monthly payment mortgage which uses a 365-day year.

The major banks in Canada offer both 360- and 365- day payment amortizations, but often don't tell you which method they are using. Before making a decision about which mortgage to accept, you should know.

One way to find out is to ask them for an amortization schedule. It will answer your question. The monthly interest factor for a 360-day schedule is constant from month to month and therefore the interest portion of the blended payment decreases consistently each period. The monthly interest factor for a 365-day schedule is dependent on the number of days from one month to the next and thus it changes each month.

In most cases the number of days per year does not have a significant effect on the overall interest cost of the mortgage, but knowing which method is being used will allow you to figure out the interest cost of each payment to the penny. That's what you need to do for effective personal financial tracking. (See Chapter 11.)

How To Save Money with Your Mortgage

Once you understand how to assess the variables in a mortgage, you are ready to calculate how you can save a lot of money by making an effective mortgage decision. The interest rate is the place to start, and that depends on the term you select.

Choose the Right Term

Generally, the longer the term of the mortgage, the higher the interest rate you are going to pay. You pay a premium to lower the risk that mortgage rates are going to rise above the interest rate you've negotiated during the term. In Canada, you can choose from variable rate, six-month, or one-, two-, three-, four-, five-, seven-, and ten-year terms.

If you choose a shorter term, you could save big. This is illustrated in Figure 4, which shows the average monthly residential mortgage rates for one-year and five-year mortgages since 1980.

David Trahair

Figure 4
CONVENTIONAL MORTGAGE INTEREST RATES SINCE
1980

DATE	1-YEAR	5-YEAR	DIFFERENCE
1980	13.98	14.52	-0.54
1981	18.13	18.38	-0.25
1982	16.85	18.04	-1.19
1983	10.98	13.23	-2.25
1984	12.00	13.58	-1.58
1985	10.31	12.13	-1.81
1986	10.15	11.21	-1.06
1987	9.85	11.17	-1.31
1988	10.83	11.65	-0.81
1989	12.85	12.06	0.79
1990	13.40	13.35	0.04
1991	10.08	11.13	-1.05
1992	7.87	9.51	-1.64
1993	6.91	8.78	-1.87
1994	7.83	9.53	-1.70
1995	8.38	9.16	-0.78
1996	6.19	7.93	-1.74
1997	5.54	7.07	-1.53
1998	6.50	6.93	-0.43
1999	6.80	7.56	-0.76
2000	7.85	8.35	-0.50
2001	6.14	7.40	-1.26
2002	5.17	7.02	-1.85
2003	4.84	6.39	-1.55
2004	4.59	6.23	-1.64
2005	5.06	5.99	-0.93
2006	6.28	6.66	-0.38
2007	6.90	7.07	-0.17
2008	6.70	7.06	-0.36
2009	4.14	5.63	-1.49
2010	3.49	5.61	-2.12
2011	3.52	5.37	-1.85
2012(to June)	3.25	5.30	-2.05
Average	8.28	9.42	-1.14
Lowest(2012)	3.25	5.30	
Highest(1981)	18.13	18.38	

Source: Bank of Canada, www.bankofcanada.ca

In Figure 4, note the following:

- The average one-year rate was 8.28 percent, and the average five-year rate 9.42 percent, for a difference of 1.14 percent;
- The lowest one-year rate was 3.25 percent in 2012, and the lowest five-year rate was 5.30 percent in the same year;
- The highest one-year rate was 18.13 percent in 1981, and the highest five-year rate was 18.38 percent in the same year.

This shows clearly that historically you pay a significant premium to stick to a five-year term. In fact, I ran the average interest rates for both the one- and five-year terms on our $150,000 mortgage, both with an amortization period of 25 years. Here's what came up:

- One-year rate of 8.28 percent: monthly payments of $1,171.74, and total interest of $201,520.13;
- Five-year rate of 9.42 percent: monthly payments of $1,283.57 and total interest of $235,067.41

The 1.14 percent interest difference would cost you $33,547.28 in additional interest – enough to keep you going back to Tim Hortons for quite a while.

The Sleep Test

Despite what you can save with a short-term mortgage, it's not for everyone. You have to be able to live with the risk that interest rates may increase. The test is the effect on your sleep. Does the thought of not locking in your rate for five years keep you up at night? If it does, keep the long- term mortgage and avoid the permanent bags under your eyes.

Payment Frequency

Many people think that if they switch from monthly payments (12 times per year) to biweekly (26 payments per year), they will save a lot of interest. That's simply not true.

Let's look at the effect on our sample mortgage (see Figure 5). The only change is the number of payments per year, from 12 to 26. The program has calculated the bi- weekly payment to be $402.20. The total

David Trahair

interest for the 26-payment mortgage is $111,432.36, compared to $111,721.44 for the 12-payment mortgage – a savings of only $289.08.

Figure 5
AMORTIZATION SCHEDULE WITH BIWEEKLY PAYMENTS

Figure 5, MORTGAGE2 PRO, copyright © 2009 is used by permission of Ron Cirotto.

Payment Amount

Simply increasing your payment frequency won't help much; increasing the payment amount will.

For example, the 12 monthly payments in our example of $872.41 total $10,468.92 in a year. If you were to make 24 payments (semi-monthly), you would pay $436.21 twice per month ($10,468.92/24). Use that amount for your 26 biweekly payments, and you are effectively making two extra payments each year. That will pay off your mortgage sooner and save a lot of interest.

Figure 6 shows the amortization schedule for 26 payments of $436.21. The total interest has declined to $93,588.65. That's $18,132.79 less than the regular monthly payment mortgage. Now you're saving money.

Figure 6
AMORTIZATION SCHEDULE WITH 26 PAYMENTS

Figure 6, MORTGAGE2 PRO, copyright @ 2009 is used by permission of Ron Cirotto.

David Trahair

Mortgage Terminology

Amortization: The gradual reduction in the principal balance owing, which happens because of the partial payments of principal plus interest at regular intervals.

Amortization period: The time required to pay off the principal balance through regularly scheduled repayments.

Blended payment: Each payment contains amounts for both principal and interest, which change over time while the overall payment remains the same.

Conventional mortgage: A first mortgage for which the amount loaned does not exceed 80 percent of the appraised value of the property.

High-ratio mortgage: A mortgage that exceeds 80 percent of the appraised value of the property. It must be insured to protect the lender in case of default by the borrower.

Interest: The amount paid by the borrower (mortgagor) to the lender (mortgagee) for the use of the money.

Maturity date: The final date in the term of the debt (not the amortization period).

Principal: The amount payable to the financial institution that gave you the mortgage. It begins with the total amount you borrow and is reduced by the principal portion of each payment.

Term: The period of time during which the money is loaned at a certain interest rate. This is usually six months or one, two, three, four, or five years.

10. Cars – Should I Lease or Buy?

Your cars are likely one of the largest expenses you will have in your life. It makes sense that you should spend some time making the decision about what kind of car to buy and how to pay for it. If you don't, you risk pouring thousands of your valuable dollars down the drain.

Let's assume for now you've picked your car and are faced with the decision to buy or lease. In Canada today, a significant number of people lease their cars. Why? Because leasing offers a significant advantage over buying: low monthly payments. But there's more to the story. Much more. Let's dig in.

How Leasing Works

Pick up the newspaper and leaf through it until you find the car ads. Try the sports section if there isn't one for cars. You'll notice that some of the ads show the cost of the car, but the majority get you focused on the monthly payment.

Hey, it's only $500 – I can carry that! The problem is that there are many other figures, and they are just as important.

Someone I know just leased a 2011 BMW 328i xDrive sedan and I have the paperwork in front of me.

Here are the details:

- Interest rate: 2.9%
- Payment type: monthly
- Term: 48 months
- Total kilometres at end: 80,000
- Cash down payment: $2,000
- Residual value (44%): $19,030
- Monthly payment (including HST): $568.62

Here is a summary of the upfront payments:

	$
Cash down	2,000.00
Rear park distance control	400.00
PPSA due on delivery	53.73
Subtotal	**2,453.73**
HST	318.98
Fuel charge	75.00
License fee	63.15
First payment	568.62
Security deposit	600.00
Total due on delivery	**4,079.48**

Residual Value

How did the dealer calculate the monthly payment amount? They got it by using an important figure – the residual value. This is sometimes referred to as the "buyback amount." It's a predetermined estimate of the value of the car at the end of the lease, and it is needed to calculate the lease amounts.

In this case the residual value is $19,030, which is 44% of the original price.

Excess Kilometre Charge

This particular car has a 20,000-kilometre-per-year limit. Any mileage over 80,000 kilometres during the four-year lease term is charged at $0.15 per kilometre. If, for example, you exceeded the limit by 10,000 kilometres, you would owe an additional $1,500 at lease end. Suffice it to say that if you may be driving a significant distance each year, leasing may not be for you.

Other Fees

What if you want to get out of the lease? There will probably be an early termination fee. There may also be a "lease service" fee. There could also be a disposition fee at lease maturity. You'd be wise to read the fine print before accepting any lease.

Types of Leases

There are two basic types of car leases. They are either "closed-end" or "open-end." Closed-end leases may also be called "walkaway" or "guaranteed trade-in" leases and open-end leases are also known as "finance" or "equity" leases. In both cases, the monthly payment is based on the term of the lease, the interest rate, and the residual value, but only the closed-end lease gives you the option of purchasing the vehicle for a predetermined price or walking away from it at the end of the term. The leasing company is assuming responsibility for the automobile's value at the end of the lease.

With an open-end lease, you are responsible for any difference between the residual value and the market value at the end of the lease. If the vehicle is worth less than the residual value, you bear the risk of paying the difference, or at least a substantial part of it. This type of lease used to be quite common but has become rare due to the hard work of some dedicated consumer advocates. Beware, however, if you get stuck with one of these: You could get hit with a substantial surprise payment at the end.

GAP Insurance

If your leased vehicle is stolen or damaged beyond repair, your insurance company will determine how much to pay you. If that amount is less than your car's "book value" (the outstanding principal and accrued interest owing on the lease), guess who pays the difference? You do. To protect you, there is a type of insurance referred to as Guaranteed Asset Protection (GAP). If you lease a car, make sure you get it. Not convinced? Think of this situation. You're two years into a lease and are involved in a serious accident. Your car is a write-off. Your insurance company pays you $15,000. The book value on your lease is $22,000.

You are left paying $7,000 to your leasing company ... and finding the money for another car.

Leasing Versus Buying

The costs to put your car on the road and keep it there can be classified in two categories: fixed costs and operating costs. Fixed costs are those required to buy or lease the vehicle. Operating costs are those needed to run the vehicle – gas and oil, insurance, maintenance, etc. Since the operating costs will be substantially the same over the first few years of a car's life whether you buy or lease, the decision comes down to a comparison of the fixed costs.

Figure 7 (on the next page) compares the fixed costs of leasing for four years versus buying the BMW 318i xDrive we just discussed.

Here are the assumptions I have used (note amounts are rounded to the nearest dollar):

Lease:
- Down payment is $2,773 ($2,453.73 plus HST).
- Additional amounts total $138 (Fuel charge plus license fee).
- Monthly lease payments are $569 ($6,828 per year).
- Residual value or end-of-lease purchase amount is $19,030.
- This is a closed-end lease with no risk of payment for the difference between the market value and the residual value.
- There are no charges for excess kilometres, wear and tear, or damage.
- There is no lease service fee.
- There is no disposition fee at lease maturity.
- GAP insurance is included in regular insurance.

Buy:
- Total cost is $47,666 (MSRP of $42,182 before tax, plus 13 percent HST).
- The amount to finance is $45,266 (the total cost of $47,666 less the required down payment of $2,400.
- Finance rate is 2.9 percent over the four-year term of the loan (same rate as the lease).
- Monthly loan payments at 2.9 percent are $1,000.

Figure 7
LEASING VERSUS BUYING

Year	2012	2013	2014	2015	2016	2017	2018	2019	Total
Year #	1	2	3	4	5	6	7	8	(Yr 1 to 8)
LEASE									
Fixed Costs:									
Cash downpayment	2773				2773				
Additional amts (fuel, lic etc)	138				138				
Security deposit	600				-600	600		-600	
Lease payments	6828	6828	6828	6828	6828	6828	6828	6828	
End-of-lease purchase	0	0	0	0	0	0	0	0	
Excess km charge	0	0	0	0	0	0	0	0	
Total Fixed Costs	$10,339	$6,828	$6,828	$6,828	$9,139	$7,428	$6,828	$6,228	$60,440
Cost in today's money			$50,335						
BUY									
Fixed Costs:									
Down payment	2400								
Principal payments	10830	11148	11476	11813	0	0	0	0	
Interest payments	1170	851	524	186	0	0	0	0	
Repairs and maintenance	0	0	0	0	1000	2000	3000	4000	
Proceeds on sale								-3000	
Total Fixed Costs	$14,400	$11,999	$12,000	$11,999	$1,000	$2,000	$3,000	$1,000	$57,398
Cost in today's money	$51,541								
CASH OUTLAY DIFFERENCE	-$4,061	-$5,171	-$5,172	-$5,171	$8,139	$5,428	$3,828	$5,228	$0
COST DIFFERENCE IN TODAY'S MONEY					-$1,206				

What the Numbers Say

During the first year, the purchase option costs exceed the leasing option by $4,061. During each of the next three years, the excess is $5,171 each year (year three shows $5,172 due to rounding). The total extra paid over the four-year term is therefore $19,575.

That's a lot of extra money to come up with, isn't it? That's why many people tend to lease their automobiles: Their cash flow simply does not allow them to buy their cars.

But to really compare leasing to buying, you have to look at the big picture – that is, the total costs over the life of the car. Let's say a good car should last for eight years before it becomes too expensive to keep it in good running condition.

In this example, the total leasing costs over the eight-year period comes to $60,466. This assumes after the first four-year lease we return the car and lease a new car of the same type and under the same terms for the last four years.

The total costs for buying are $57,398 assuming the car is sold for $3,000 after the eight-year period. You'll see I have also estimated the repairs and maintenance costs of $1,000 in year five, $2,000 in year six, $3,000 in year seven and $4,000 in year eight. These estimates are the key to the comparison – what are the repairs going to cost you? If you are confident you can pick a good car and therefore it will have low repair costs, go ahead and buy it and keep it as long as you can.

If you are not so sure and don't want to take the risk of expensive repairs and possibly driving an older less reliable car, consider leasing. That is a major advantage to leasing – you will always be driving a relatively new car that should be under warranty.

The excess costs of leasing versus buying over the eight years in this example are only $3,048.

That's useful information, but to truly compare the leasing versus buying costs it's necessary to discount the future cash flows into today's dollars. This is done to account for the fact that a dollar today is worth more than a dollar at a future time. For example, if you could earn 6 percent interest a year in a bank account and you had $1.00 today, it would be worth $1.06 a year from now, since it would grow by 6 percent. Discounting is the reverse of that. $1.06 a year from now is worth only $1.00 today when discounted at 6 percent. In other words, the present value of $1.06 received a year from now discounted at 6 percent is $1.00 in today's dollars.

The calculations in Figure 7 have been done for the leasing and buying options at a rate of 6 percent. As we have seen, the total leasing costs are $60,446 but in today's dollars it's $50,335. For the buying option, total costs are $57,398 and in today's dollars that is $51,541. The difference is only $1,206 higher for the lease option. Effectively you have spent that much more over the eight-year period in today's to be driving a newer car during years five to eight.

Calculate your own figures the next time you need to replace your car. It's easy: Just use the Car Lease versus Buy Analyzer that you can get free from my website at www.trahair.com.

A Word about Interest Rates

An important factor in deciding whether to lease or buy is obviously the interest rate.

In the example I have assumed the interest rate is the same low rate for leasing and buying. If the lease rate were only 5.9 percent per year, however, the monthly lease costs would rise to $579 a month or $654 with taxes at 13 percent. That would total $7,848 per year, representing an increase of $1,020 over the annual lease costs with a 2.9 percent lease rate ($7,848 − $6,828 = $1,020).

If the loan rate were 5.9 percent, the loan payments would increase decrease to $1,061 per month or $12,732 per year. That would be $61 a month higher than the loan at 2.9 percent.

Don't get too caught up in the mathematical details. Just be aware of the fact that the interest rate should be a significant factor to consider in your next decision about leasing versus buying.

How to Save Money

Buy and Keep Your Car Longer

To discuss this idea we need to deal with something called depreciation. Depreciation (or amortization) is simply the amount of value that is lost over a period of time. For example, if you buy a widget and it lasts for ten years and then is worth nothing, it has depreciated by 100 percent over the ten years. The key point is that depreciation is usually not a consistent thing. The widget doesn't lose 10 percent of its value for ten years in a row. Depreciation is usually faster in the beginning and slows down over time. This is the case with cars. Often they lose up to 50 percent of their value in the first three years.

A $50,000 car will lose approximately $25,000 in the first three years and then be worth $25,000. During the next three years, however, it may lose as little as 15 percent of its value. In this case, that's only $7,500. So after six years the car is still worth $17,500 ($50,000 – $25,000 – $7,500 = $17,500). This is an important point. If you lease every three years you are paying for half of the car's value while it depreciates by the same amount. If you bought the car, over the next three years you would be paying for the other half of the car's value but it only depreciates by $7,500. You are ahead by the difference: $17,500. That is the real cost of leasing a new car every three years - you pay for 100 percent of the depreciation.

It therefore makes economic sense to consider buying a car and financing it over a longer period of time, say five or even six years. This would keep the monthly payments lower, but doesn't give you as much flexibility as the lease option. For example, say your lease car gave you a lot of problems in the first three years, or your family situation changed and you wanted a different type of car. It's easy with the right type of lease -you just give the car back.

Buy a Less Expensive Car

Spending less money on your next car is another obvious way to save yourself thousands of dollars.

Maintain the vehicle well and keep it for a few more years and you'll really be saving money as long as the repairs and maintenance costs don't quash your plans.

Think of your monthly cash flow after you have that car paid off in four years. During each of the next payment-free years you'll have thousands of dollars more cash available – that's the monthly lease payments you won't have to make.

What is the downside, apart from the fact that you are driving a less expensive car? As mentioned, maintenance costs will obviously be higher on an older car because more parts will need replacement. However, these costs probably won't come close to the savings achieved by buying and keeping a less expensive car.

Buy a Used Car

Buying a used car is one way to drive the car you want for a reasonable price but you need to be very careful.

Used Car Warning

In researching this issue, I was fortunate enough to find an expert on car leasing and buying. His name is Bob Prest, and he was instrumental in helping me clear away the smoke and mirrors surrounding car leases. He shared the following advice that could save you thousands of dollars and countless headaches.

Be careful if you buy a vehicle that is two years old or newer. Very few people trade in a car that is under two years old because they would be taking such a big financial loss on depreciation, as discussed above.

So why would someone sell his or her car after only two years? Bob gives three reasons. It has been:

1. A daily rental with hundreds of drivers before you;
2. Used as a service vehicle with many drivers and careless maintenance; or
3. In an accident (the most common reason).

If you buy a car that is less than two years old, get a written statement from the dealer that the vehicle was not a daily rental, not a service vehicle, and has not been in an accident. If a dealer won't give you such a letter for any reason, do not buy the car and do not do business with this dealer. If you get the letter, you can force the dealership to take the vehicle back if it turns out they hid the truth.

This is one of the reasons that in his business as a car broker, Bob only finds new vehicles for clients to buy or lease. For further information, visit Bob's website at www.dealfinder.org.

David Trahair

Summary

The main advantage to leasing is that it allows you to drive a new car for a low monthly payment. If you can control all the variables, including potential hidden fees and charges, this may be the answer for you.

If, however, you are looking for areas in your personal financial life where you can save thousands of dollars, consider buying a less expensive or used car and keeping it longer.

11. Tracking Your Finances: The Ultimate Weapon

Most people are very sloppy with their personal finances. They pay their bills and credit cards late, they rush major financial decisions, and their investments languish due to a lack of attention. This kind of behaviour leads to:

- Loss of thousands of dollars in needless interest and other charges,
- Mounting debt levels,
- Poorly performing investment portfolios,
- Increased risk of a major financial meltdown, and
- Ruined retirement dreams.

Your financial affairs don't have to follow this pattern. You can take control, stop the hemorrhaging, and begin to build a solid financial future. Unfortunately, it's not going to be easy, and it won't happen quickly. It takes years for most people to get into this kind of mess; it will take more than a few months to get out of it.

The best way that you can take control of your finances is to spend time tracking and analyzing them. I call this "personal financial tracking."

Personal financial tracking is the process of recording all income and expenses that your family brings in and pays out during the year as well as all the changing asset values and debt balances. Put simply, it's bookkeeping for your personal life.

It is no different than what any business must do. To succeed, a business needs accurate bookkeeping records of what has happened in the past and where it stands at the moment. In fact, every business is required to do this kind of bookkeeping in order to file income taxes.

It's really no different for personal finances. You have to report your income, but if you are employed, that is done for you by your employer on an annual basis. All you have to do is file your T4 slip with your personal income tax return. If you are self-employed, your business revenues and expenses must be reported.

The problem arises with your personal expenses. There is no outside force demanding that you track them, so if you're like most people, you probably just don't do it; and that's a huge mistake. If you don't know where the money is going, it's very difficult to spot and plug the big money leaks.

Of course, most people don't deliberately set out to get themselves into a financial mess. Tracking your finances takes time and commitment, and often there just doesn't seem to be enough hours in the day. For most people, life is busy enough with work and the demands of a family. Even those with the best intentions rarely get around to spending much time on their personal finances. Many conclude that working harder to make more money will solve their financial problems. The result is that they have even less time available for what really matters in life, while excessive spending sucks the life out of their finances.

Often, another roadblock is that the information needed is disorganized or even missing. Without an efficient filing system, you're pretty well doomed from the start. I have dealt with hundreds of people over the years, and I usually find some consistent traits: Those who have all their accounting records organized and on time one year usually do it every year. Those who are disorganized remain that way.

Unless you are very disciplined and organized, you are unlikely to naturally make positive changes. You need some motivation to start tracking, and that's not hard to find. If you start tracking your finances, odds are you'll find *at least* one area that is wasting your money. If you identify and plug one money drain, you could end up saving thousands of dollars.

At the very least, start a folder for each area of your personal finances: bank statements, RRSP statements, credit cards, and loans. That way, you can locate information to make some basic decisions. Maybe you will decide to move a balance from a gold credit card at 19 percent to a line of credit at 7 percent, or maybe you'll plan a vacation in Canada this year rather than an excursion to the South Pacific. Perhaps you'll buy a used car after your current lease expires.

Add up the savings, and it could work out to an after-tax windfall of thousands of dollars for several hours' work.

Take my own example. Many years ago, I decided to get serious about tracking my own personal finances. I tried for months to get myself to do it. I had the software, the motivation, and our family records filed neatly. I just couldn't bring myself to start. I remember thinking that the last thing I felt like doing after a hard day's work analyzing clients' financial statements was cranking up the computer and filling up my spare time with a bookkeeping exercise.

What actually got me going wasn't any lofty goal; it was the motivation of money. I thought to myself that I would gladly pay someone, probably a bookkeeper, $100 per month to enter all our personal financial information into a spreadsheet program. Then it struck me: if I could learn how to do this efficiently, it could be a service that I could provide for a fee. That's when I buckled down and developed the system I describe in this chapter.

Tracking Hotspots

You can make your personal financial tracking easier if you recognize – and address – the hotspots. Those are the daily expenses that may seem small at the time, but can add up to huge amounts. These kinds of expenses are also very easy to forget about, and so they may not get tracked at all.

Expenses paid by cash are the most vulnerable to being "lost," and cash withdrawals are one of the biggest problems for people trying to bring their finances under control. How many times have you withdrawn $50 or $100 from the ATM and been shocked a few days later when there's nothing left in your account? If you don't know where your money is going, you will find it very difficult to reduce or stop the outflow.

Unless you are a sucker for punishment and enjoy keeping receipts for every little thing you buy in cash and then summarizing them later, use a debit card for as many expenses as possible. The payee's name will be included on the bank statement for every transaction, saving you the time of figuring out where your money went. Even if you don't remember exactly what the details of the transactions were, at least you will know which organization the money went to, and you'll be able to make an educated guess about in which expense category it belongs.

I also suggest that you write cheques whenever possible instead of using cash. Although not as easy as using a debit card, paying by cheque does provide a trail for your tracking purposes. For example, if you pay someone to cut your lawn, suggest paying by cheque instead of cash. When the bank returns your cheques with your monthly statement, you can record the expense appropriately.

David Trahair

Personal Financial Tracking Options

There are two methods for tracking your finances:

1. The quick-and-dirty method

2. The detailed tracking method

Let's look at each in turn.

The Quick-and-Dirty Method

The quick-and-dirty method is the easier of the two, but is the least useful. Unfortunately, it's the method used by the majority of people who try to track their finances. Here's how it works:

Step 1: List your assets

First you list the balances of your assets as of a particular date. You can do this quite easily. Simply gather all your bank and investment statements, and estimate the value of your other assets, including your home, cars, and property (e.g., summer cottage), and list them all as of the same date. Use a month-end date, such as December 31. For your convenience, you can download a worksheet from my website at www.trahair.com. It's called the "Net Worth Calculator."

Step 2: List your liabilities

The next step is to summarize the balances of all the amounts you owe as of the same date. Gather all credit card, mortgage, and other loan statements and list the amounts under your liabilities on the spreadsheet.

Step 3: Calculate your net worth

Now subtract your total liabilities from your total assets. What you're left with is your net worth.

Step 4: Record your monthly income and expenses

Now you need to list your monthly income and expenses. To do so, you can use another spreadsheet you can get from my website called the "My Income and Expenses." It is Worksheet 2 at the end of this chapter. You enter the monthly amounts, and it will multiply by 12 to get the annual totals.

If you are on salary, your income figure is easy to determine: it's your net monthly pay. If you are self-employed, list the average amount you transfer each month to your personal bank account.

Listing your expenses accurately is the most difficult part of using this method. Some expenses are easier than others to determine. For example, you may have consistent monthly withdrawals for things like your mortgage, insurance, car payments, etc. Most other expenses, however, have to be estimated, and that is where problems can arise. Estimates are only guesses, and guesses are not a solid base from which to plan your financial future. For that reason, the quick-and-dirty method is the least accurate one to use.

The Detailed Tracking Method

This method tracks every dollar coming in and going out, which results in detailed reports of your spending and net worth. While it requires you to invest in a financial software program, the cost is easily offset by the time savings.

Having monthly details is far superior to estimating an average month and simply multiplying by 12 to get annual amounts. Because your finances will probably vary significantly from month to month, basing your annual estimate on one month will likely give you a false picture of what you are actually spending. Recording accurate historical information about your monthly spending will enable you to spot the cash drains. If you just guess, you are leaving those drains open.

The main software choice available is Quicken by Intuit. This program is designed to track personal finances and offers the following major advantages:

- You can automatically download bank and credit card information from your bank.

- You can generate extensive reports, allowing you to analyze things from a myriad of different angles.
- Automatic entries can be set up to save time.
- There are built-in loan amortization schedules.
- There is a built-in personal rate of return calculator for investments.
- Automatic double entry bookkeeping connects the cash flows to the related net worth accounts.

Downloading the Transactions

Having the ability to download your banking information over the Internet directly to the program will save you a lot of time.

Before you begin, you'll need to sign up for the service with your bank and select a password. Here are a few hints for effective tracking:

- Limit the number of bank accounts you have.
- Set up your credit cards for downloading as well.
- Always compare the balance in the bank account and credit card statement to the printed copy you receive in the mail to make sure you didn't miss anything.

A high-speed Internet connection is not imperative, because the download files are small. If you receive a message about the download being unsuccessful, just click through, as it often works anyway.

The Main Reports

The software will provide two main reports: the net worth report and the cash flow report.

The cash flow report shows you the amount of cash inflows and outflows during a period of time. The software program can either combine all sources, including bank accounts and credit cards, or it can "filter" the report to just show certain sources. It does all the work for you.

One of the most important reports is the cash flow comparison report. It gives a detailed listing of all income and expense categories for one period compared to another and calculates the amount difference. It is here that you will be surprised and possibly motivated to act by some of the categories. It is also here that you will experience the great feeling of making progress, as you increase income and decrease expense amounts.

It's important to note that the cash flow report includes transactions from all bank, cash, and credit card transactions, but excludes transfers between these accounts. For example, a transfer of $1,000 from your bank account to your credit card will not show on this report, nor would you want it to, as it is not an income or expense item but merely a transfer from one balance sheet account to another. The transfer will, of course, be reflected on the net worth statement, as the balance in your bank account and credit card accounts will have gone down by $1,000.

Investments

Unfortunately, unless you have an extraordinary broker, investment information won't be easy to enter, because you usually won't be allowed to download your information. Financial advisors also rarely show the cost of investments on monthly statements for reasons we have previously explored.

You will need to dig through your past files to find out how much you paid for each investment. Take the time to do this. If you don't, the reports on your investments will probably be misleading, and with your retirement at stake, you can't afford to be misinformed.

Separate Amounts into Components

It is very important to separate lump-sum payments into components. If you don't do this, you will get a skewed view of your expenses.

For example, your mortgage payments will have several parts. You need to separate the interest component (an expense) from the repayment of principal (a cash outflow that reduces a liability). The payment may also include property taxes (an expense).

The distinction is important, because the repayment of debt is quite different than the payment of either interest or property taxes. The repayment of debt is the progress you are making on getting out of debt. It reduces your liabilities on your statement of net worth.

To separate the principal reduction, you'll need an amortization schedule of the mortgage. You may have received one from your financial institution when you first took out or renewed your mortgage. If not, an amortization software program will do the job for you (see Chapter 9).

Salary Deductions

The best way to deal with salary and employment income is to show the gross amount, and then list all the deductions separately. Doing so will provide you with the details on how much the various withholdings, such as income tax, CPP, and EI (Employment Insurance), are costing you.

Interest

You should record interest expenses in a separate category for each loan. Doing so will make it easier to analyze your debt situation by highlighting exactly where the interest charges originate. You can then target and reduce the worst offenders first. When credit card interest stares you in the face for months on end, you may decide to do something about it!

Business Expenses

If you are self-employed, create a separate category for expenses related to your business, even if you have a separate business bank account and bookkeeping records. There are many expenses that you incur personally which can also be claimed as business expenses, including automobile, meals and entertainment, and a home office. If you don't track these expenses, chances are they'll be missed, and that means you'll pay more tax than you should. Tracking also makes tax time easier for your accountant because the information is nicely summarized.

Children

You probably didn't decide to have kids based on a cash flow projection, but tracking how much they cost can help you to control these significant expenses. Make sure you separate the figures, such as before- and after-school programs, trips, camp, etc. Again, if you can't see these numbers, you'll find it difficult to keep them under control.

Household Expenses

I suggest grouping together all home-related expenses. Doing so will give you the figures you need for any home office deduction to which you may be entitled (if you have self-employment income), and it will also give you an overall snapshot of how much your home is costing you. Consider categories for furniture, insurance, mortgage interest, property taxes (or rent), electricity, heating, repairs and maintenance, security, and anything else you may have.

Insurance

Keep tabs on all types of insurance, including separate entries for life and disability insurance for you and your spouse. Insurance relating to personal and business automobiles, house, and business insurance should be placed under those categories.

Projecting into the Future

Tracking provides information about your past income and spending, but if you are to make changes, you need to look to the future. Quicken provides budgeting and cash flow features, but I have found them to be difficult to use. However, there is a solution. Simply export or copy the data to a spreadsheet such as Microsoft Excel.

The advantage to having your data in a spreadsheet is flexibility. It's easy to move things around and add columns where needed. If you are not familiar with spreadsheets, I urge you to take a course on it. Once you learn how to use one, you'll find many uses for it in addition to budgeting.

Obviously, the first year is the toughest because you won't have any historical data on which to base your projections. Wait until you have at least a month or two of data in your file before doing any projecting. It's best to project your figures on an annual basis.

David Trahair

How to Use the Projection Spreadsheet

Have a look at Worksheet 3 at the end of this chapter or the "Cash Flow Projector" spreadsheet from my website. It will allow you to estimate your income and expenses for the rest of the year.

You will note that I have put income taxes and other deductions right under the gross income amounts on the spreadsheet, since doing so makes it easy to see the net amount available to spend. That is the figure that you need to keep in mind when you budget.

You will see several columns, as follows:

- **Column B.** Actual figures for the prior year: These will come from your My Income and Expenses spreadsheet or your Quicken cash flow reports.
- **Column C.** Actual figures from January 1 to a certain date (March 31 in this example): This is the actual money you earned and spent during the first quarter (or other period) of the current year.
- **Column D.** Estimated figures since the date in column C to December 31: Here you should use the figures you entered in column C to help you estimate what they will be for the rest of the year.
- **Column E.** Estimated figures for entire year: The sum of columns C and D is calculated automatically.

Assume you have entered all your income and expense data in Quicken from January 1 to March 31 of this year. Display the cash flow report for that period and either copy, export, or type in the actual totals into column C of the cash flow projection spreadsheet. Don't worry about column B for now. That's for the results of a prior year, once you have them.

Projecting the cash flows for the remainder of the year (column D) is made easier by the spreadsheet. Many income and expenses are monthly items, so if you have, say $180 in telephone expenses for the first three months of the year, put in triple that amount, $540, for the remaining nine months.

Hint: Put in a formula for the amount and copy to other categories that act the same. The formula is =C10/3*9 for the remainder of the year estimate if cell number C10 is the cell containing the $180 for three months' telephone expense.

Aim to update your personal finances at least every three months. Trying to do it more often will be time consuming and I have found it won't really help much. If quarterly updates take too much time, try updating every six months. If you leave it for a year or more, it'll be too late to make any changes until the next year.

The main thing you will notice when you track your spending is that you probably have a significant amount of discretionary expenses – those things that aren't absolutely necessary. For example, you may see that those luxury car leases or that extended vacation are the easiest expenses to target and cut. Once you have detailed information on hand about your spending, you'll most likely be very surprised at the amount of money you can save.

A Few Words about Killer Credit Cards

As I have said over and over, if you spend more than you make on a consistent basis, your financial situation will get worse and worse each day. Credit cards give you the instant ability to buy things that you can't afford. It's all so easy, but it can be deadly.

A gold card offering free air miles or merchandise may sound like a great deal, and it is, unless you don't pay off the balance in full by the due date. Interest rates of 19 percent up to 28 percent or more for some department store cards are common. The spending habits of many Canadians have given credit card companies a licence to print money, and they are experts at convincing you to load up the plastic.

Nonetheless, if you can afford to pay off your credit cards each month, they offer some great features.

If you find that you are too easily lured by the convenience of credit cards, try this: simply switch from a credit card to a debit card. This strategy will automatically limit your spending to what you have in the bank, plus any overdraft protection. I guarantee this will be tough if you carry a credit card balance from month to month, but the alternative is to keep spending more than you make by borrowing from the credit card company.

The use of credit cards is becoming an epidemic, with some companies even mailing out approved cards that have not even been requested, as well as targeting young people without jobs. Credit cards can be lifesavers, but they can also suck the financial life right out of you. Your best bet is to become educated about the traps.

The Financial Consumer Agency of Canada (FCAC) is an independent body started in 2001 to protect and educate consumers of financial products. Their website at www.fcac-acfc.gc.ca has a tremendous amount of useful information.

The comprehensive credit card comparison tables on this website are definitely worth a visit. They compare all the costs and details of many different types of cards (standard, gold, platinum, etc.) from most of the financial institutions in Canada. That's independent, objective information you aren't going to get anywhere else. They even have a toll-free number you can call for financial advice. Try it at 1-866-461-FCAC (3222) [in English] or 1-866-461-ACFC (2232) [in French].

They offer the following tips to help you save money with credit cards:

- Don't base your credit card decision on one factor such as the introductory rate or reward program. Look for the overall package that best suits your needs and financial situation.
- If possible, pay your entire balance in full each month. If you cannot pay the whole amount, transfer the balance to another form of credit with a lower interest rate such as a line of credit. If you do this every month you will benefit from the grace period on the card.
- If you carry a balance on a credit card, remember that interest is normally charged from the date a purchase is made until it is paid in full. Making early payments between statements will save you interest charges.
- Cash advances should be made only when absolutely necessary – for short-term or emergency situations, since interest is charged from the date you borrow until the advance is paid in full.
- Allow enough time for your payment to reach your credit card company.
- Consider the use of pre-authorized payment plans to automatically make your payments on time. You will need to keep track of such payments to make sure sufficient funds are in your account.

- Monitor your monthly statements for notices of fee increases or rule changes from your credit card company.

If you are carrying a balance on a gold or premium card charging you around 20 percent annual interest, you need to take action as soon as possible.

One option is to switch to a low-rate card. It's as easy as a phone call, in many cases. This switch will immediately save you around 10 percent a year in interest payments. The next step is tougher. How did you get here in the first place? You must have spent more than you earned over a period of time.

If you don't change your ways, even with a lower-rate card, the interest charges on an ever-increasing amount of credit card debt will eat your retirement dreams alive. The first step is to control yourself so that you are spending only what you make every year. Doing that will be tough, but it's the only way to stop the balance from rising.

David Trahair

Worksheet 1
NET WORTH STATEMENT

My Net Worth Calculator Results for: *0*

Net Worth Calculation Date: *2012-12-31*

MY NET WORTH STATEMENT

ASSETS	**$**
Cash and Bank Accounts	
Chequing account	*0.00*
Savings account	*0.00*
Total cash and bank accounts	*0.00*
Other Assets (market value)	
Principal residence	*0.00*
Cottage	*0.00*
Main car	*0.00*
Second car	*0.00*
Total other assets	*0.00*
Investments (market value)	
Business value	*0.00*
Investments outside RRSP	*0.00*
RESP	*0.00*
RRSP	*0.00*
RRSP – Spouse	*0.00*
Total investments	*0.00*
TOTAL ASSETS	*0.00*
LIABILITIES	
Credit cards and Lines of credit	
Main credit card	*0.00*
Other credit cards	*0.00*
Lines of credit	*0.00*
Total credit cards and lines of credit	*0.00*
Other liabilities	
Principal residence mortgage	*0.00*
Cottage mortgage	*0.00*
Main car loan	*0.00*
Second car loan	*0.00*
Prior year personal taxes	*0.00*
Total other liabilities	*0.00*
TOTAL LIABILITIES	*0.00*

Worksheet 2
INCOME AND EXPENSES
MY INCOME AND EXPENSES
Version 91105

	MONTH ($)	YEAR ($)
INCOME		
My net pay		0.00
Self-employment income		0.00
Spouse's net pay		0.00
TOTAL INCOME	**0.00**	**0.00**
EXPENSES		
Auto		
Fuel		0.00
General		0.00
Insurance		0.00
Lease		0.00
Licence & registration		0.00
Loan interest		0.00
Maintenance		0.00
Total auto	**0.00**	**0.00**
Business		
Advertising		0.00
Auto fuel		0.00
Auto insurance		0.00
Auto lease		0.00
Auto loan interest		0.00
Auto maintenance		0.00
Auto parking		0.00
Auto other		0.00
Dues & subscriptions		0.00
Internet		0.00
Loan interest		0.00
Meals & entertainment		0.00
Office & general		0.00

David Trahair

Total business	**0.00**	**0.00**
Children		
Child care		0.00
Daycare		0.00
Holiday & camp programs		0.00
Lessons		0.00
Private school tuition		0.00
Trips & other		0.00
Total children	**0.00**	**0.00**
Family		
Cash withdrawals		0.00
Clothing		0.00
Donations		0.00
Entertainment		0.00
Gifts Given		0.00
Groceries		0.00
Vacation		0.00
Total family	**0.00**	**0.00**
Household		
Furniture		0.00
Insurance		0.00
Mortgage interest		0.00
Property tax		0.00
Repairs & maintenance		0.00
Rent		0.00
Total household	**0.00**	**0.00**
Insurance		
Disability		0.00
Life		0.00
Life -- spouse		0.00
Total insurance	**0.00**	**0.00**
Interest and bank charges		
Bank charges		0.00
Credit card interest		0.00
Line of credit interest		0.00
Personal taxes interest		0.00
Total interest and bank charges	**0.00**	**0.00**
Medical		

Dental		0.00
Medical		0.00
Private health care		0.00
Total medical	**0.00**	**0.00**
Other Expenses		
Legal & professional fees		0.00
Recreation		0.00
Restaurants -- personal meals		0.00
RRSP admin fees		0.00
Subscriptions		0.00
Miscellaneous		0.00
Total other expenses	**0.00**	**0.00**
Utilities		
Cable TV		0.00
Cleaning		0.00
Electricity		0.00
Gas & oil		0.00
Lawn & driveway		0.00
Security		0.00
Telephone		0.00
Water		0.00
Total utilities	**0.00**	**0.00**
TOTAL EXPENSES	**0.00**	**0.00**
INCOME LESS EXPENSES	**0.00**	**0.00**

David Trahair

Worksheet 3
CASH FLOW PROJECTION

**CASH FLOW
PROJECTOR
Version 100606**

	Actual cash flow of previous year	Actual cash flow of period this year	Estimated cash flow for the rest of this year	Estimated cash flow for entire year (Column C + D)
	20--	1/1/20-- to 3/31/20--	4/01/20-- to 12/31/20--	20--
INFLOWS				
Salary (gross)				0.00
Interest income				0.00
Other income				0.00
Salary of spouse (gross)				0.00
TOTAL INFLOWS	**0.00**	**0.00**	**0.00**	**0.00**
My tax				
CPP contributions				0.00
EI contributions				0.00
Income tax				0.00
Pension				0.00
Total my tax	**0.00**	**0.00**	**0.00**	**0.00**
Spouse tax				
CPP contributions				0.00
EI contributions				0.00
Income tax				0.00
Pension				0.00
Total spouse tax	**0.00**	**0.00**	**0.00**	**0.00**
Total tax	**0.00**	**0.00**	**0.00**	**0.00**
My net pay	**0.00**	**0.00**	**0.00**	**0.00**
Spouse net pay	**0.00**	**0.00**	**0.00**	**0.00**

Net other	0.00	0.00	0.00	0.00
NET INFLOWS	0.00	0.00	0.00	0.00

EXPENSES

Auto

Fuel				0.00
General				0.00
Insurance				0.00
Lease				0.00
License & registration				0.00
Loan interest				0.00
Maintenance				0.00
Total auto	0.00	0.00	0.00	0.00

Business

Advertising				0.00
Auto fuel				0.00
Auto insurance				0.00
Auto lease				0.00
Auto loan interest				0.00
Auto maintenance				0.00
Auto parking				0.00
Auto other				0.00
Dues & subscriptions				0.00
Internet				0.00
Loan interest				0.00
Meals & entertainment				0.00
Office & general				0.00
Total business	0.00	0.00	0.00	0.00

Children

Child care				0.00
Daycare				0.00
Holiday & camp programs				0.00
Lessons				0.00
Private school tuition				0.00
Trips & other				0.00
Total children	0.00	0.00	0.00	0.00

Family

Cash withdrawals				0.00

Clothing				0.00
Donations				0.00
Entertainment				0.00
Gifts given				0.00
Groceries				0.00
Vacation				0.00
Total family	**0.00**	**0.00**	**0.00**	**0.00**
Household				
Furniture				0.00
Insurance				0.00
Mortgage interest				0.00
Property tax				0.00
Repairs & maintenance				0.00
Rent				0.00
Total household	**0.00**	**0.00**	**0.00**	**0.00**
Insurance				
Disability				0.00
Life				0.00
Life — spouse				0.00
Total insurance	**0.00**	**0.00**	**0.00**	**0.00**
Interest and bank charges				
Bank charges				0.00
Credit card interest				0.00
Line of credit interest				0.00
Personal taxes interest				0.00
Total interest and bank charges	**0.00**	**0.00**	**0.00**	**0.00**
Medical				
Dental				0.00
Medical				0.00
Private health care				0.00
Total medical	**0.00**	**0.00**	**0.00**	**0.00**
Other Expenses				
Legal & professional fees				0.00
Recreation				0.00
Restaurants — personal meals				0.00

RRSP admin fees			0.00
Subscriptions			0.00
Miscellaneous			0.00
Total other expenses	**0.00**	**0.00**	**0.00**	**0.00**

Utilities

Cable TV			0.00
Cleaning			0.00
Electricity			0.00
Gas & oil			0.00
Lawn & driveway			0.00
Security			0.00
Telephone			0.00
Water			0.00
Total utilities	**0.00**	**0.00**	**0.00**	**0.00**

TOTAL EXPENSES	**0.00**	**0.00**	**0.00**	**0.00**

TRANSFERS

TO Mortgage	0.00	0.00	0.00	0.00
TO Investment a/c 1	0.00	0.00	0.00	0.00
TO Investment a/c 2	0.00	0.00	0.00	0.00
TO RESP	0.00	0.00	0.00	0.00
TO Business loan	0.00	0.00	0.00	0.00
TO My RRSP	0.00	0.00	0.00	0.00
TO Spouse's RRSP	0.00	0.00	0.00	0.00

TOTAL TRANSFERS	**0.00**	**0.00**	**0.00**	**0.00**

TOTAL OUTFLOWS **(Expenses + Transfers)**	**0.00**	**0.00**	**0.00**	**0.00**

NET INFLOWS LESS **TOTAL OUTFLOWS**	**0.00**	**0.00**	**0.00**	**0.00**

12. Summary: What You've Learned and What to Do Next

Now that we've exploded the top five myths about financial planning in Canada today, you're in a better position. Simply knowing what the myths are is an important first step in your quest to gain control of your finances and enjoy the trip to retirement and beyond.

Let's review the key points of each myth and the counter arguments to each.

Myth 1: If I Had $1,000,000 ... I Could Retire

The rule of thumb says you'll need at least 70 percent, perhaps even up to 100 percent, of your pre-retirement income after you retire, and that means you will need to save more than $1 million before you get there. Here's what we discovered as we took a journey with the Harts:

Reality: If you get control of your finances and retire debt-free you probably won't need 70 percent, because you won't have the same level of expenses and you won't still be putting away money for retirement.

You'll have at your disposal funds from your RRIF (converted from your RRSPs) as well as CPP and OAS to rely on. As well, if you manage to pay off your home mortgage, you've secured an excellent way of providing for your future. If you control your expenses and pay off all personal debt, you may need as little as 40 percent of your current income to retire comfortably.

Myth 2: RRSPs Are the Holy Grail of Retirement

Ask your average investment advisor about retirement, and he or she is likely to immediately jump into a discussion about your RRSP and how the stock market is the place to be, even if you have to borrow to invest. You'll likely be told how RRSPs can save you lots in taxes, too.

Reality: Investing in RRSPs gives you a tax deduction now, but you have to pay tax on the withdrawals later. If your tax bracket is not much lower after you retire, the savings may not be much at all. The real advantage to RRSPs is that they defer tax. That can be a real economic benefit, and that's one of the reasons why investing in RRSPs should be a part of your retirement planning – after all debt, including your mortgage, is paid off.

Borrowing to invest in an RRSP is not wise. The only winner is the bank.

Myth 3: Don't Worry about Your Investments You'll Be Fine in the Long Run

The stock markets can give you a good return on your money. All you have to do is pick the right time to get in and the right time to get out.

Reality: Choosing the right time to buy and sell in the stock market is almost impossible. You need to be very lucky to get it right. You're gambling with your future if you're counting on the stock market to provide you with your retirement funds. Use the personal rate of return calculator that is available from www.trahair.com to figure out how well the stock market has done for you in the past before trusting it in the future.

Myth 4: We Have Met the Enemy, and He Is the Tax Collector

Paying taxes is a distasteful chore, but you can avoid paying more if you just pick the right tax shelter and use leverage to buy into a great investment.

Reality: It doesn't make economic sense to invest $10,000 in a tax shelter to save $4,600, if there is little chance of getting your original investment back. If you don't get it back, you have just burned $5,400.

It could even get worse if the government discovers that your tax shelter is a scam. Using "leverage" to get rich is as risky as it gets. You borrow money and hope that the returns will exceed the tax-deductible interest on the debt. You could get lucky and beat the odds, but you may very well end up broke if you choose the wrong investment or simply get the timing wrong.

Myth 5: Secure Your Financial Future Buy Life Insurance

Everyone needs insurance, and you can kill two birds with one stone if you invest in a policy that includes savings features.

Reality: Insuring the life of the breadwinner in a family is a prudent step in personal financial planning. If he or she was to die, any dependents would be left with no means of sustaining themselves. However, insuring the life of someone who does not contribute economically to the family finances or someone without dependents is probably not necessary. Whole life insurance means a whole lot of commission to your insurance agent. That is one of the reasons why it is not a great way for you to save money. And your savings, otherwise known as the cash surrender value, help fund the death benefit. You don't get the cash surrender value and the death benefit; you get one or the other.

You don't have to fall for these myths. You now have at your disposal the tools and information you'll need to defend yourself against those who wish to relieve you of your hard-earned money. You can use a business calculator to test investment projections and loan alternatives. You can work diligently to pay off what is probably your biggest personal debt: your home mortgage. And you can start using the ultimate weapon: personal financial tracking, the key to your financial well-being. If you can get yourself motivated to track your finances, you are armed and ready to defend yourself.

What Now?

Okay. You're not going to fall for any of the myths, you're committed to doing your own personal financial tracking from now on, you're going to attack all personal debt and pay it off as soon as possible, and you've successfully cut your expenses to the bone. What next?

Since you now pay your credit cards off in full each month, get the card with the most rewards for what you need and start using that card. It's like getting a free loan and being rewarded for taking it. Just don't fall into the trap. The credit card pit can be mighty deep, and it has very slippery walls.

Since all your debt is paid off, you'll have a lot of excess cash each month. Begin investing in earnest. Decide the best amount to put into your RRSP using the retirement optimizer available for free from my website at www.trahair.com. Spend time educating yourself about investing.

Oh, and take that dream vacation. You've earned it!

Iguana Books
iguanabooks.com

If you enjoyed *Smoke and Mirrors*...
Look for other books coming soon from Iguana Books! Subscribe to our blog for updates as they happen.

iguanabooks.com/blog/

You can also learn more about David Trahair and his upcoming work at www.trahair.com.

If you're a writer...
Iguana Books is always looking for great new writers, in every genre. We produce primarily ebooks but, as you can see, we do the occasional print book as well. Visit us at iguanabooks.com to see what Iguana Books has to offer both emerging and established authors.

iguanabooks.com/publishing-with-iguana/

If you're looking for another good book...
All Iguana Books books are available on our website. We pride ourselves on making sure that every Iguana book is a great read.

iguanabooks.com/bookstore/

Visit our bookstore today and support your favourite author.

IGUANA

CPSIA information can be obtained at www.ICGtesting.com
Printed in the USA
LVOW10s0007081114

412599LV00002B/2/P